THE NEWPORT HARBOR MURDERS REVISITED:

THE CRIMINAL JUSTICE SYSTEM FOUND GUILTY

BY

BROOKS W. WILSON

In honor of the Overell, Jungquist and Rector families,
all stalwart families who deserved much better than betrayal.

PUBLICATIONS BY BROOKS W. WILSON

Cost analysis of certified tuition courses - 1971

The P.O.S.T. training program: a review and critique - 1972

Police discretion as public policy - 1973

An analysis of the role of the training officer in California law - 1973

The growth and development of the California Commission on Peace Officer Standards and Training - 1974

Course evaluation instrument project: final report - 1974

Training needs assessment survey – 1976

Residential construction management - 2005

A Mormon's View of the 20th Century: The rise and fall of the american middle class - 2011

TABLE OF CONTENTS

PREFACE

When I was a young lad of 17, I was captivated by this case. I lived about 60 miles away in Fontana and followed the pretrial and trial in the papers. Louise Overell was born seven days after I was and just a few miles away. I felt a bizarre connection to her. Every afternoon, I would get off the school bus at the corner of Arrow and Sierra, borrow the Los Angeles Examiner and read about Bud and Louise, then put the paper back. I read every word that was written in the Examiner. I was certain they would be convicted. The newspaper writers were certain they would be convicted. When the verdict came in, I was shocked. More than the verdict, however, the reaction of the public shocked and even angered me. While following the O.J. Simpson case and upon hearing another surprise verdict and miscarriage of justice, I was reminded of Bud and Louise. A few months back, while doing some research for another book, I stumbled upon a brief mention of this case and decided it would be interesting to write about it. There have been several brief articles written about it in the 64 years since the murders but covering only the surface… just enough to whet my interest.

This is a true story. The characters are real and the events are well documented. In some cases where the character is still alive and use of the real name may cause embarrassment or where there may be an invasion of their privacy, fictitious names are used. There are just a few and they are foot noted. The book uses actual family names. As in any historical account, descendants are still alive. It isn't a docudrama because my opinion is clearly expressed. It can be considered a critique of the trial, the attorneys and the American Justice System. Hopefully, it is informative entertainment. It is an interesting story.

The only part of the book that is fiction is the dialogue inserted in an effort to give life to the cold history. Content of the conversations are based on personality of the characters as gleaned from the testimony at the trial, investigation reports, contemporary newspaper accounts, and the letters written in the Orange County Jail by the two defendants; for the most part the conversations took place in actual events.

The primary purpose of this book is to entertain. The criticism of the system, the investigators, witnesses and attorneys is sincere. It is based on the review of the investigation reports, trial transcripts, and my experience as a policeman; along with considerable research. Psychological analysis of the defendants is not intended as expert but is based on common sense along with some peripheral research which is documented. Again, this book is intended for entertainment but truth is usually more entertaining than fiction; the book is true!

A search of genealogical records of the Rectors and Jungquists, along with extended members of their families was made to get a feel for the families. These are solid families and it is perplexing how Bud Gollum and Louise Overell could have morphed into something, an evil unit, which could have done something that is so discordant with the life that was offered them. Hopefully, this book will offer an explanation.

The main text of the book includes a complete unedited set of all the letters or notes exchanged by Bud and Louise while in jail awaiting trial. Much of it amounts to poorly written pornography and I feel somewhat uncomfortable including it. But, in my opinion, the letters and notes are vital to understanding their character and the dynamics of their relationship. For those who are sensitive, I have included the edited version printed at the time in the Los Angeles Examiner which you can read instead of the unedited versions.

ACKNOWLEDGMENTS

I was overwhelmed with the cooperation and assistance I received in researching the book.

Sergeant Jay Shorts, of the Newport Police Department, did an exhaustive search of their records for information on the crime which took place in the city limits of their city. Sergeant Shorts found nothing but it was helpful in turning me in a different direction. If he had not made his effort, I could have spent more time in a fruitless search.

County Archivists located at "The Old Orange County Courthouse," now retired as a museum, located a gold mine. They possess the complete transcripts of the entire 101 day trial; over 1500 pages. They brought out six boxes of transcripts, gave me a place to work (Chris pointed out to me that I was working at the desk the attorneys used at the trial) and Susan even copied some pages for me. My thanks to Susan Berumen, who confided that she had the best job in the county, Chris Jepsen, Steve Ostelie and to Marshall Duell, the retired Curator of the Old Orange County Courthouse Museum.

Kris, who handles requests for records for the Orange County Sheriff's Department, provided me with virtually everything from their files on the Overell murders. This included some invaluable investigation reports.

The State of Alaska Department of Public Safety provided me with the arrest report of Bud Gollum in the town of Palmer, Alaska.

The Howard Gotlieb Archival Research Center in Boston University provided me with a complete set of typewritten letters between Gollum and

Overell written while in the Orange County Jail awaiting trial. This is probably the only copy of this material extant.

Ancestry.com through which I found many old newspaper articles covering the individuals involved in the crime, investigation and trial.

\

Part I

CRIME, INVESTIGATION AND PRETRIAL

A merica was a good place to be in 1947. America was just gearing up for the post war boom. The first television station west of the Mississippi went on the air in Hollywood – KTLA-TV. Jackie Robinson became the first Negro, as they were called then, to play in major league baseball. Chuck Yeager became the first supersonic flyer when he broke the sound barrier. UFO's were invented or discovered. The house Un-American Activities Committee set up shop in Hollywood and Howard Hughes took the wooden airplane, the Spruce Goose, up for its first and only flight.

Sugar was 85 cents for 10 pounds, milk was 78 cents a gallon, bread was 13 cents a loaf, a new house cost $6650, average income was $2,854 a year, rent was $68 a month, a movie ticket cost a half dollar, gasoline was 15 cents a gallon and stamps cost 3 cents. There were plenty of jobs and it was easy to go to college. Things should have been good for a young discharged sailor with GI benefits from a well-to-do family and his rich and intelligent young girl friend.

Newport Harbor is in the incorporated city limits of Newport Beach. The weather in Newport Beach is almost boringly pleasant. The yearly average high temperature is 68 degrees and the low is 56 degrees. Only four months, July through October, does the high temperature edge into the low 70s. The lows edge down into the high 40s in December and January. Average annual rainfall is 11.65 inches with no month getting as much as 3 inches. You might say that if you bring a jacket you are dressed appropriately for Newport Beach.

The rest of California was caught up in the post war growth associated with the burgeoning middle class and growing prosperity. While Newport got a bump in growth of 173% between the 1940 and 1950 censuses, with most of that probably coming after the war, the population was still small and Newport Beach never really had a middle class. The middle class was relegated mostly to the neighboring cities of Huntington Beach and Costa Mesa. Crime in Newport Beach was pretty much what residents read about in the papers; and it took place in neighboring Los Angeles County and to a lesser extent in North Orange County cities.

Although it has grown and become crowded, Newport Harbor is still beautiful. In 1947, the population of Newport Beach was less than 10,000 and the natural beauty was even more striking without the crowded housing and increased traffic.

THE CRIME.

On March 15, 1947, at 11:45 PM, the weather was probably between 50 and 60 degrees on a typically starry night. Walter E. Overell, 62, and his wife Beulah, 57, were aboard their 47 foot Yacht, the Mary E, which was moored in the harbor, when an explosion aboard shattered the still of the night and sent the yacht to the bottom of the shallow harbor while many of the residents were either in bed asleep or about to go to bed

The Explosion was heard by Newport Beach police officers Lawrence Goddard and George W. Calihan who were on patrol in the area. They saw the boat sinking and called the fire department. The two officers saw Bud and Louise running hand in hand near Bay Avenue and A Street. The boat was boarded at 11:52 P.M. by Robert Myers of the Newport Beach Fire Department and he found the bodies of Walter and Beulah Overell. Members of the Coast Guard arrived shortly and took the bodies to the Baltz Mortuary. At this point, murder was not suspected. The boat marked with the X in the picture depicts the approximate location of the Mary E when it exploded.

Officer Goddard later talked to Gollum at B Street and Central Avenue (marked B in the picture). Louise was sitting in her parents' car. The police allowed the young couple to row out to the boat where they were sent back. Gollum asked the officers what he should do. "Louise is very much upset, we are engaged to be married, I would like to take her home, would that be possible?" Gollum ended up taking her home in his own car, a light green 41 Pontiac coupe. Instead of taking her to Grandmother Jungquist's home where she would be around family and mutual grieving, he took her to the vacant mansion in Flintridge where they were alone.

Police investigations would lead to the later arrest of the Overell's 17 year old daughter, Louise, and her boyfriend George Bud Gollum who had been aboard earlier but were on shore at a late night café when the explosion occurred.

The Overells lived in the upscale unincorporated city of Flintridge, now LA Canada/ Flintridge, located in the foothills north of Pasadena and Glendale. It is a small city with a population of 20,000. It was once noted for having the cleanest air in Southern California. Flintridge has a colorful and somewhat checkered

past. Before WWII, it was the gathering place for the American German Bund, a Nazi sympathizer group with ties to Hitler. After Pearl Harbor, it became the home of a Japanese American internment camp in the Tuna CCC camp.

In 1947, the Overells were among the many wealthy residents. Walter was born in Evansville, Indiana on August 23, 1883 and Beulah Ann Jungquist was born in Riverton Iowa on June 10, 1890. The two were married on June 2, 1914 in Los Angeles. Walter had made a modest fortune in the furniture manufacturing business and later in successful real estate investments. Beulah was a leading socialite in the small town of Flintridge and was erroneously rumored to have had an affair with one of the developers, ex-Senator Frank Putnam Flint who named a street after her. Beulah Louise was the Overell's only child. She was born when her mother was 39 years old. There is, or was, an unproved belief that children born to women late in life have an inherent problem and while there is the common belief that an only child is usually a spoiled child, there is no evidence to prove that Louise was a problem child. If, however, Louise was guilty of murdering her parents, or being complicit in the murder of her parents, one could certainly make the case for her having the symptoms of an over-indulged child. She was a first year journalism major at the University of Southern California at the time of the murders.

THE INVESTIGATION.

The initial assumption was the explosion was an accident resulting from fumes of a leaky butane tank but the coroner reported that victims could have been dead up to an hour before the explosion. The boat was pulled into shallow waters and the investigation resumed. The butane tank was found to be sound and there was no fire which would have been present in a gasoline explosion. Newport Fire Chief Frank Crocker, investigating the suspected fire, found a wire leading to a detonating cap and 30 unexploded sticks of dynamite which are shown in the picture above attached to a time clock and the ship's clock records the exact time of explosion.

The bulkhead was splintered and Walter Overell was impaled on one of the broken boards. Both Walter and Beulah had suffered skull fractures that could not have been caused by the explosion and investigators began suspecting murder; the circumstantial evidence pointed to Bud and Louise. Questioned by the police, they stated that they had been on board earlier but had rowed ashore to get some milk and hamburgers at 11:00 PM, 45 minutes before the explosion. When they realized what had happened, Bud and Louise told police, they ran to the wharf where they were seen by the two NPPD officers. The account given of the earlier evening by the young couple raised the suspicion of the investigating officers

On March 17th, Coroner E. R. Abbey, ordered Dr. Larry Mathes to perform an autopsy at Baltz Mortuary. Both Walter and Beulah, as stated above, had severe head wounds that wouldn't have been caused by the explosion. These were listed as the cause of death. Two days after the trial started (three months after the murders), during jury selection, a second examination was made by Dr. John J. Montanus at the insistence of Otto Jacobs, Louise's attorney. His conclusion was the same, more or less, as the first one. The explosion did not cause the deaths.

On March 19, Sheriff Musick and Captain T. R. McGaff, commander of the Bureau of Records and Identification, having been given the keys to Gollum's car inspected the automobile. The following is part of his investigation report of March 19, 1947:

> "At about 3:00 P.M. Sheriff Musick and Capt. McGaff went to Los Angeles in the 4600 block of Santa Fe Avenue and found George Gollum's Pontiac coupe, Lic. 3M 7307 with 1946 tags attached to rear license plate parked in the parking area at the Percival Steel Company. We found wires attached to the car at the bottom of the dash board to the left of the steering post attached to a small button type switch which was similar in color and appearance as the wires attached to the electrical detonators taken from the boat; also flesh colored adhesive tape in the glove compartment, small side cutters used to cut wires, sleeping tablets and misc. articles. From the rear of the car, we found a lap robe which appeared to be splattered with blood, a bundle of men's clothing identified by Gollum as being his blue navy work shirt, light colored slack pants, pair black navy type shoes, and blue woolen men's socks in the shoes, all containing what appeared to be blood spots except the woolen socks.

> 'We also found large coils of multi-colored bell or radio type wires, some coils were of solid color, the ends of the wires had at some time been attached to other or different type of wires approximately the same size at (sic) the bell wire, also three or four small radio type batteries.

> 'At about 5:00 P.M. we also had a conversation with the housekeeper for the uncle[1] who lives on Manhattan St., Los Angeles, regarding an alarm clock described as a large one that was in Louise's room at that residence, and that this alarm clock had failed to ring a couple of times causing Louise to be late for school, and that the uncle had to go upstairs after that and wake Louise, and that Gollum had brought her an electric alarm clock, and that she has not seen the old alarm clock since; and that on March eighteen[th], 1947, Louise and Gollum came to the house and moved practically all of Louise's belongings to her Flintridge home."

---

1 Fred Junquist

THE ARREST.

Meanwhile, investigators from the Orange County Sheriff's Department and the Newport Beach Police Department were preparing a probable cause case against Bud and Louise for murder. They were asked by Sheriff Musick if they could meet him at Chief Hodgkinson's office at the Newport Beach Police Department while they were there picking up the Overell Car which had been towed in for safe keeping. Bud and Louise met Emmanuel Jungquist at his steel company, Percival Steel, on Santa Fe Avenue in Los Angeles. They parked Bud's car there and drove to Newport Beach with Emmanuel.

Gollum met Sheriff Musick and Chief Hogkinson in the Chief's office. When Sheriff Musick was asked about the conversation as a witness at the trial, this was his response:

> "I asked Mr. Gollum how he and Louise had traveled to Newport Beach that morning and he told me that they had stopped by the Percival Steel Company and there met a Mr. Jungquist and came down in Mr. Jungquist's car leaving his car parked on the parking lot at the Percival Steel Company. I asked him to describe the automobile and he said it was a light green Pontiac Coupe, I believe he said it was a 1941 model. I am not positive of that but that it was parked on the parking lot at the Percival Steel Co. I asked him if he locked the automobile and he said that he did."

Sheriff Musick asked Bud to give him the keys and he did voluntarily. Later, he and Captain McGaff drove up to L.A. and found the incriminating evidence listed earlier in Bud's car. With all this evidence, Sheriff Musick and Chief Hodgkinson, in spite of resistance by the Orange County District Attorney James Davis, arrested and booked George Rector Gollum and Beulah Louise Overell for suspicion of murder.

The Arrest reports and booking sheets are no longer in the Orange County Archives. The logs shown here are the only documents in their records relative to the booking. These log items provide the essential information found on booking sheets. They chronicle the fact that on March 19, 1947, George and Louise were booked under 836.3 of the California Penal Code for suspicion of murder. On March 27, 1947, they were rebooked on a bench warrant issued through a Grand Jury indictment. The log includes other miscellaneous information relative to their booking. There is a notation on George Gollums log indicating that he was sentenced to prison on March 10, 1950 in a federal prison for transporting a stolen car across state lines.[2] Also illustrated by these logs is the fact that DA Davis was not aboard on the prosecution and is why Chief Hodgkinson requested a prosecutor from California Attorney General Fred Howser.

```
                    OC# 22577     17 W 000 20
    OVERELL, Beulah Louise          17 U 000 19


FWA brn green 5'6" 135 17-47 nat. Calif.

3-19-47  Viol.836 Sec.3 PC (Murder)     Arr 74343
3-27-47  Bch War.-Grand Jury Indictment on Murder
                                         Arr 74455
3-22-47  Anonymous phone call            DR-5038
3-25-47  Teletype #1 LSH (CASE #636)     DR-5038




                    OC# 22578     9 U 100 16 Rf. T
    GOLLUM, George Rector           18 T  OI 15      T


MWA blonde blue 6'1" 220 21-47 nat. California

3-19-47  Viol.836 Sec.3 PC (Murder)     Arr 74342
3-27-47  Bch War.on Grand Jury Indictment on Mur-
         der                             Arr 74456
3-22-47  Anonymous phone call            DR-5038
3-25-47  Teletype #1 LSH (CASE #636)     DR-5038
3-10-50  Fed.Corr.Inst.Tallahassee,Fla.#7606-TF-
         N.M.V.T.A.(Transporting)
```

The arrest came four days after the murder. Although she was eligible for bail, Louise remained in jail partly because she said she wanted to remain close to Bud, who was remanded, but probably mostly because her attorney wanted to keep her available for consultation. It was learned that the couple had planned to get married on her eighteenth birthday on April 30th but prosecutors refused to let the wedding go on. Most likely, they planned to wed when she turned eighteen because her parents could no longer prevent it.

---

2 The notations on the log are esoteric. The author knows what the charges were from investigation into Gollums life after the trial.

The police investigation intensified after the arrest. Formally or informally, the responsibility for the investigation was assumed by the Sheriff's staff.

On April 20th, Sgt. Harry Lace and Captain McGaff boarded the Mary E at the South Coast Boat Works where it had been impounded. They found a ballpeen hammer in the bathroom of the front cabin. It was consistent with the wounds on Mrs. Overell's head. They also found a long pipe that had been removed from the apparatus which holds the life boat for the Mary E.

The next day, they found blood stained tennis shoes and clothing which was later identified in County Jail by Gollum as being his. Gollum told McGaff and Chief Hodgkinson the blood stains were from the nose bleed that his girlfriend Louise had some time ago while on the beach. He further stated that he had smelled a strong odor of gasoline all day and presumed the gasoline was leaking. He said that after taking the mechanics ashore, Mr. Overell returned and told him and Louise to go ashore for sandwiches and milk and to bring his car keys from his car. He said they left the boat about 11:00 P.M., ate their hamburgers and bought a hamburger and some milk for Mr. and Mrs. Overell. When they were returning they heard the explosion. Later that day, Sheriff Musick, McGaff and Chief Hodgkinson questioned Louise back at the jail about the clothing. She was not sure but thought the clothing might belong to Bud. She said she had nose bleeds sometimes but the last one she could remember having was at Bud's parents' home and that she had never had a nose bleed while at the beach.

The Overell's house keeper, Mrs. Pritchett identified two keys that Gollum had in his possession when he was arrested as belonging to Mrs. Overell and that she never let anyone take her keys and always had them in her possession. She further stated, quoting Captain McGaff's report, "that immediately after the accident, Gollum and Louise came home to Flintridge and completely ransacked the house, opening all  drawers in every room, throwing things on the floor and scattering clothing, papers and boxes about the rooms."

Earlier, probably around the time of arrest, infighting developed, most likely over jurisdiction and control of the investigation, between Newport Beach Chief Rowland R. Hodgkinson and District Attorney James L. Davis. Orange County Sheriff Jim Musick[3] became very much involved in the investigation and sided with Chief Hodgkinson. Sheriff Musick, who had been a football star at USC and with the old Boston Redskins, was a newly elected sheriff, but he had paid his dues as a deputy before and after serving as an officer in the Marine Corps during the war. Davis was an attorney and a politician. District Attorneys are evaluated by their conviction rate. This was obviously going to be a high profile case and he did not want a failure in the national spotlight. On the other hand, Hodgkinson and Musick were cops. They deal with the victims and are characteristically more aggressive than prosecuting attorneys. In addition, the chief was unhappy with the amount of information being given the press by the DA's office.

Gollum and Overell had not been arrested on a warrant initially. On the 19th of March they were arrested on reasonable cause. They were indicted by the grand jury on the 27th. District Attorney Davis was hesitant to file an "information"[4]. He was annoyed when he found out that the two had been arrested on suspicion. He felt he was being pressured by Chief Hodgkinson and Sheriff Musick. In fact, he was. He asked them to meet with him in his office and they agreed. When they were seated, he looked at the sheriff and then the chief and said, "What the hell is going on, chief?

Hodgkinson had been chief of police for nearly 20 years and was not intimidated by Davis who was first elected in 1943.

"If you're talking about the Overell case, Jim and I feel that we have an obligation to the community. We feel we have an open and shut case."

"Everything you have is circumstantial. You have no physical evidence," Davis retorted in a somewhat condescending tone.

Musick, only 37 years old at the time was an imposing figure. He not tall, about 5'10", 200 pounds, with gray wavy hair, a broad suntanned face, a broad

---

3 Photo courtesy Orange County Archives

4 In California, there are two ways a defendant can be brought to trial. One is by being indicted by the grand jury and the other is by the district attorney filing an "Information" outlining the charges. It's easier to get a grand jury indictment than to convince the DA to file so law enforcement agencies sometimes use the grand jury. The conviction rate is much lower with indictments.

nose and prominent chin. He just looked tough. But he was soft spoken and a gentleman. He had only been sheriff for a year but he was no neophyte. He had spent years on the department as a deputy and had worked the streets. He had lived in Santa Ana most of his life. Sheriff Musick spoke up:

"Mr. Davis," he said respectfully, "We have wire taken from his car that matches the wire used on the detonator on the boat; we know that the explosion was not the cause of death, Gollum and Louise were on the boat with them just before the explosion. They claim that Overell sent them ashore to get sandwiches but they were about to leave to go home. It doesn't add up. Why wouldn't they all leave and eat together after closing up the boat? We have Gollum's bloody clothes taken from his car which we feel certain will prove to be the blood of one or both of the Overells. With them in jail awaiting trial we have time to gather more evidence. This was an amateurish murder and there is evidence out there."

Davis was not convinced. "Well, I'm not going to file and information. You'll have to get a grand jury indictment."

They shook hands and the chief and sheriff left the office. Chief Hodgkinson was seething. The next day, he contacted Fred N. Howser, the Attorney General for the state and requested that Davis be replaced with a special prosecutor because of "constant leakage of the people's evidence and the lack of vigor on the part of the District Attorney." The AG, probably anxious for the publicity of a high profile trial, complied by hiring Eugene Williams as a Special Prosecutor. The chief was also probably looking forward to some notoriety. Williams brought some of his investigators with him which added some confusion in fixing responsibility. Sheriff Musick, however, as low key as he was and with less experience than any of the others quietly took over. The investigation continued.

On March 28th, Chief Hodgkinson brought in three packages tagged as evidence by Sgt. Harry Lace of the Newport Beach Police Department. The content of one package was a blood stained board taken from the boat. The other two were wires found on the boat by Sgt. Lace. The blood stained board was important. Larry Pinker of the LAPD would later testify that the blood had to have been on the board at least 20 minutes before the boat sunk or the water would have washed it away. The blood type was the same as Walter Overell. This reinforced the prosecution's claim that the Overells were killed before the explosion.

At 5:15, the same day, Sheriff Musick, Chief Hodgkinson and DA Davis, soon to be replaced, presented Captain McGaff with a receipt for 50 sticks of dynamite purchased from the Trojan Powder Company in Chatsworth. It was a cash purchase of $16.05 and was signed by R. L. Standish giving an address of 206 West Blvd, Palmdale. It was also signed by Robert Comstock. The salesman was L. A. Hill. McGaff compared the signatures on the receipt with handwriting cards submitted by Gollum and Overell at the time of their arrest and stated that he believed the signatures on the receipt were Gollums. He was told that C. A. Hill would be in his office the next day for the purpose of identifying Gollum and Overell. Hill, however, when he came in was unable to state positively whether Gollum and Overell was or was not the couple that had made the purchase.

Later, investigators went to the Palmdale post office and substation and determined that there was no such address as 206 West Blvd. and there was no one by the name of R. L. Standish or Robert Comstock living in that postal district.

Sometime in late March, Ben Smith, Deputy Sheriff Jailer for the San Bernardino Sheriff Department, contacted investigators and reported that he may have sold some dynamite to Gollum and Overell. He operated a business called the Powder Magazine. He recognized them from the pictures he had seen in the newspapers when they were arrested. Mr. Smith also operated a gasoline station in San Bernardino. On April 2nd, he came to Captain McGaff's office for the purpose of positive identification. From Captain McGaff's report:

> "At approximately 10:30 A.M., Mr. Ben A Smith, Deputy Sheriff of San Bernardino County and operator of the Powder Magazine at San Bernardino, came to the office for the purpose of identifying Gollum and Miss Overell as being the persons making the purchase of dynamite on or about March 2nd, 1947. In the presence of Deputy Stahl and myself (sic) he was taken to the Identification Room and Gollum was brought in. I engaged Gollum in conversation while Mr. Smith watched and listened to his manner of speech, posture, etc. We then took Gollum back to the jail. After taking Gollum back downstairs, Mr. Smith state that he thought Gollum was the person who made the purchase.

> 'Mr. Smith was then taken to the Women's Jail where he saw Louise

Overell and he stated that he was sure that the girl was one of the party the day the dynamite was purchased. He again related his conversation with the purchaser as having the tape around the stick so that the water would not leak in, and about the dynamite being used for stumps, and that the stumps were located in Santa Ana and the ground was rather hard and again explained the methods he told the purchaser to use in dynamiting.

'At 1:15 P.M., Deputy Stahl, Deputy Smith and myself (sic) left the office for the South Coast Boat Works, Newport Beach, aboard the "Mary E" for another inspection. Deputy Smith having about fifteen (15) years' experience in handling dynamite gave an estimate at the approximate amount of dynamite used in the explosion. Then after carefully examining the two holes in the boat, he estimated that about forty (40) to fifty (50) sticks were used in the forward cabin where the hole is located near the toilet and engine room door, and that the sticks were lying on top of the floor boards in the forward cabin and that possibly some heavy object might have been lying on top of the sticks because of the nature of the hole and the twisted condition of the wood at that point and that ten (10) sticks or more may have been used in the engine room appearing there to be the lessor amount of damage and also the type of damage at that location. He stated that the sticks that had failed to explode might have failed due to their being too far away from the one connection to the cap and as a result of being too far apart the exploding sticks had no effect on the others. It merely blew them around the bottom of the boat."

McGaff took a formal signed statement from Deputy Smith declaring that he had sold 24 sticks of dynamite along with six (6) four feet exploders to George Gollum and Louise Overell on March 2nd.

Investigators contacted classmates of Gollum, Philip Edward Mason and Lester James Nelson, Jr. Nelson had been a longtime friend of Gollum in the Boy Scouts as well as in school. Nelson told investigators that Gollum had told him that Louise's parents objected to the marriage and threatened to cut her off if she married him. Mason said that when he asked Gollum what he saw in Louise that he referred to the South West Bluebook which listed only millionaires. Gollum said that Walter Overell was listed in it.

Mason stated that other members of the class heard him.

Members of the Overell family were interviewed and they reported behavior of the young couple that was inconsistent with the grief that would normally be displayed. They were reported to be playing ping pong both at the Flintridge mansion and at the home of Louise's cousin. A neighbor, Mrs. Herbert Van Zwoll was interviewed and stated (and later would testify), that Louise asked her to spend the night at the Flintridge home the night after the accident, and was awakened early in morning by Gollum and Louise laughing and that she saw Gollum searching Mrs. Overell's bedroom, opening drawers. She told police that she saw him hand Louise a fur coat that she later wore to the Overell funeral after she was arrested.

The prosecution had their case.

1. The Overells were killed by blunt force that was unlikely to have been caused by the explosion.

2. They were dead when the explosion occurred and the boat was flooded.

3. Louise and Bud were with them, the only ones with them, just before the explosion.

4. They had purchased dynamite on two separate occasions, the most recent purchase taking place on March 14th, the day before the murders.

5. Walter Overell had threatened to cut Louise off from her inheritance if she married Bud.

They had the motive, the weapons and Gollum and Louise were the only ones who had the opportunity. No one else could possibly have done it. It looked like an easy win.

Chief Hodgkinson got his way and Eugene Williams was hired as special prosecutor. Williams had gained a reputation for being good with "circumstantial evidence" by successfully prosecuting Japanese war criminals after the war. He would learn that popular opinion was on his side with the war prosecutions and would not be on his side against the young couple in this case. Otto Jacobs and Z.B. West represented Louise and Gollum hired

S.B. Kaufman and William Beirne. The way it turned out, Jacobs was all the pair needed.

Years later the Santa Ana Register, now the Orange County Register, reported that "she (Louise) was a menopause baby, apparently unwanted, misunderstood and unloved; an ugly duckling daughter." She was pudgy at five feet, six inches tall with dark hair and bushy eyebrows.

Her boyfriend, George Rector "Bud" Gollum was a navy veteran and a loner. He was born on March 1, 1926 in Los Angeles to Fred W. Gollum and Wilhelmina Rector Gollum. Gollum had a sister, Wilifred Gollum (nicknamed Pete), two years older than him. Fred Gollum was a well-to-do stock broker. The 1930 census showed they lived in census district 73 in a $20,000 home and had a live in maid. Gollum and his sister attended Los Angeles High School. He was a fairly good looking young man with short blond hair and chiseled features. He was 6'2" tall and weighed 220 pounds. He wore rimless glasses and had what some people might consider the appearance of an intellectual. According to most reports at the time of the trial, he was not well liked. He was three years older than Louise. They had become acquainted through correspondence encouraged my members of the families while he was still a radioman in the navy.

Both Overell and Gollum came from large families although she was an only child and he had just one, older, sister. Gollum's mother divorced Fred Gollum and married Dr. Joseph Stomel sometime between the 1930 census and Bud's affair with Louise. Dr. Stomel had five children by his deceased former wife.

To a policeman, as stated earlier, this would seem like an open and shut case. The young couple was alone with them on the boat earlier. They were the last visitors. No one else could possibly have done it. The cause of death was blunt force injury to the head; injuries that the explosion did not cause. The only issue in doubt, it would seem, would be the pattern of participation. How were each involved in the actual act. It also seems like trying them together was a mistake. Separating them would open up the possibility of working one against the other instead of solidifying their defense. Ironically, the defense wanted them separated and the prosecution wanted to try them together. The only possible alternative to their being the murderers was an accident. Williams chose to try them together, presumably because it would be difficult to prove which one actually did the killing. By trying them together, he would not have to prove the specific involvement of either; he would have to prove by circumstantial evidence that "they" killed them.

The prosecutors were undoubtedly aware that they would have to convince 12 people beyond a reasonable doubt (Mr. Williams would find out that the real foe was to be unreasonable doubt) that two young people who seemingly had everything could do the unbelievable; murder both parents of one of the couple's by crushing their skulls with a hammer and pipe. Looking at it as an observer, it is difficult to fathom. What could possibly bring these two young people to do such a horrible thing?

Murder of parents by children is not as unusual as one may think. A study in Australia shows that there has been nearly one a day over a ten-year period:

> "Psychologists have debated for years whether family violence is caused by the same factors as general violence. In the 1980s, the US clinical psychologist Edwin Megargee - one of the most respected US authorities on criminal violence - concluded that family violence resulted from special factors such as psychological distress rather than material gain or increased status. However, other researchers have found "street crime" influences such as greed can motivate a child to kill a parent.

> "We don't want to believe it is possible," says the forensic psychiatrist Dr. Rod Milton. We want to claim it is [mental] illness rather than merely depravity. The deed proves the madness: No sane person would do such a thing.

> "But Milton believes psychiatrists and judges too readily accept such explanations. Judges fall over backwards to be sympathetic to people who murder their parents. Psychiatrists and criminologists tend to suggest three main reasons children kill those who gave them life: mental illness or disorder; neglect or abuse; or psychopathic tendencies."[5]

In studying the case of George Rector Gollum and Beulah Louise Overell as a couple one can see all three of the elements, mental disorder, neglect

---

5 http://www.smh.com.au/articles/2004/10/13/1097607298969.html

and psychopathic tendencies as well as greed.

There were love letters or notes passed between Bud and Louise and delivered by jail personnel that somehow got into the hands of the Los Angeles Examiner and were published in their newspaper.

THE LETTERS/ NOTES.

On April 29, 1947, the day before Louise's eighteenth birthday, the Los Angeles Examiner printed this story:

> ### State Sees Break Between Overell Girl and Gollum
> **Santa Ana,** *April 29__*
> *Existence of More Letters Disclosed*
> *Possibility of a "break" between Louise Overell and George (Bud) Gollum was anticipated by Attorney General Fred N. Howser today. The Attorney General appeared here today following exclusive publication in the Examiner of a series of passionate letters exchanged by Bud and Louise in the County Jail.*
>
> *Howser disclosed existence of further unpublished correspondence between the college sweethearts awaiting trial on murder charges May 26th and said:*
> *"I hope these unpublished letters haven't fallen into the hands of anyone. They contain what I believe may amount to serious admissions, although not confessions, on the parts of defendants.*
>
> ### 'May be a break_____'
> *The tenor of these letters leads me to believe that there may be a break between the defendants before they go to trial" the Attorney said and concluded that "lurid, unprintable, sexy passages in these notes can be expected to influence continued investigation. They may be important in trial of this case.*
>
> *Louise, who will be eighteen this year, and her, and her twenty-one year-old boyfriend are accused of killing the girl's wealthy parents, Walter E. and Beulah, blown up in the families power cruiser at Newport Harbor last March 15.*

In jail since last March 19th, they believed that they had won the sympathy of guards who carried the notes between their cells.

Notes filed.

Actually, authorities have been aware of the exchanges from the beginning. Each note was photographed before delivery and became a part of prosecution files. Publication of the letters by the Examiner brought sharp reaction from both sides of the bench (inaccessible)... end of article.

———

There were later statements, not under oath, that Attorney General Howser leaked them to the Examiner. Some of the notes were so lurid that Judge Kenneth Morrison deleted some of the language. After the trial, Judge Morrison ordered them burned. Fortunately, all the copies weren't burned. After an exhaustive search, the author located type written copies of all the letters/notes at the Howard Gotlieb Archival Research Center of Boston University.

The letters are graphic and lurid. They are undoubtedly X-rated; the reader is advised before reading any further. The author feels it is vital to provide them in their unedited form to make a clear depiction of the nature of the couple tried for murder. An edited version, as gleaned from the internet pictures of the articles in the Los Angeles Examiner is provided in the appendix.

It is not clear from the notes exactly when they began and the sequence is somewhat tentative. They started around the 12th of April and the sequence is fairly accurate given the possibility of a few of the notes being lost. Considered all together, in or out of sequence, they paint a graphic picture of the tentative and waning nature of their relationship at that time. The letters are presented exactly as written. Grammar and spelling errors are included:

Saturday

4-12-47

Started about 7:00 AM

Baby mine,

    First an apology for that last night's note. I'll explain that. Remember how you felt about that telephone conversation with Miss Ricks that time at your house? Well, I felt that way last night. Because of the remark you made "Mr. Jacobs might be a competitor if he liked me in other ways than as a client." Does that mean it's all up to him? You already like him and are waiting for him to say the word. I had hoped, from your first letters that he was just an employee and not a personal friend. Am I mistaken?

    You said that you don't remember what the medical examiner did." Knowing you as I do, I am of the opinion that merely means that you don't want to tell me. Why, I don't know. I thought we were going to tell each other everything. But, still, if you don't want to, it's O.K. We'll not mention that any more. This certainly sounds very self-righteous doesn't it?

    If you haven't drawn those diagrams as yet you can forget them. I think I have the idea up to the door at the top of the steps, and when I see you in court, I'll ask you about the rest. Just one thing. Please do draw a diagram showing the way from your cell to the elevator. I think that you have been in it. N'est ce pas? Please use the edge of the envelope to draw the lines with.

    I love you my darling. I adore you. Perhaps that is why I got so mad. If I did not care I wouldn't have said or written a word. I got in a fight last night. Don't say anything to Jacobs or <u>anyone</u> though. I did not get hurt. He has a black eye.

    I'm sorry I got so mad at you, but do you realize that if we are found guilty, I get killed. I don't want to die. I have to live for you, honey. And I am going to live for you and with you. That is why the knowledge of the layout of that portion of the jail is so important. If we have to do <u>that thing</u>, we will have only one chance. No more. And we'll have to make good the first time.

Here's what I think it looks like from the main door on your floor. Is there a small barred window in it? Where is the door form the kitchen into your place? Where is the elevator?

Please draw the route to your cell from the elevator.

I love you my dear, I adore you.

Here I go pulling a trick typical of me. Telling you to forget the diagrams and then asking you to draw them. I would very much like to know about the way from your cell to the elevator. All of the door and what kinds, etc. Bell, buzzers, etc. Will you please also take notice if any of the male guards open the doors up there? Take note of the matron's habits. Does she sleep in that door? When a girl is brought up do they call from below stairs? Please note all of the little things possible my dear.

Do you mind if I call you baby? Or Baby doll? How about after you have a baby or six. Will you mind me calling you baby then? Don't believe all those stories about a woman being "wicked" only once and having a child. We will have many, many child(s) my dear. And they will all be beautiful like you. Talk about wearing junior out, <u>hunh</u>. I am going to wear Butch out you mean. There are 24 hours in a day – figuring 2 hours for Junior to recover, that'll be 12 times a day. O.K? Will that be alright with you? With Butch? Can I try? Did bruise you yesterday? Please answer that.

This, instead of a self-righteous letter is trying hard to be one of abject apology. If you were here I would kiss your big toe for you, several times.

<u>Please answer all the questions in this letter.</u>

In Argentina you can get a two-inch-thick T-bone steak with two fried eggs and potatoes for 50 cents. Buenos Aires is the third largest city in the Western Hemisphere. Over 3 million people. Their pesos are equal to 25cents US money.

Your engagement ring is all paid for by the way. This will go on in the morning. It's about 12:00

———

Hi, stupe, pops, darling!

I sure miss you. I adore you. Otto tells me I won't want to marry you after the trial. So I bet him and I don't lie to lose a bet.
The relatives, Marjorie, Yvonne, and Little Fred were here. They brought me a malt. Can you do leather tooling down there, weave etc.?

Please darling do something.
I miss you so much I adore you. I dream of your big beautiful chest – darling pops, no one will ever have a beautiful (and hairy) a chest as you, Pops, I don't want any other man, the thought is revolting. I want you.

There's so much I want to tell you, and but there's not time nor space.
I miss you, I love you so much. Pops, I don't care if you are after only my money, large laugh or what else, as long as I've got you faithful, that's all I care about.

I miss you, sweetheart, so much. It gets so bad every once in a while. And when I don't feel good, I just lie there, in my bed, and whisper your name, and how wonderful you are.

Darling, you haven't gotten in any more fights, have you? It worries me a lot. Please get started on something. Darling, should I ask to go out on bail. I wouldn't get to see you or write to you. I wish you had your sox. Damn Otto anyway. I want to see you so much. I miss your hair, and your wonderful nose, and your teeth, and your glasses, oh, all of you. I miss you calling on the phone, I miss you being irritated for my being late. I miss Catalina and you being there. I miss from July 4 to March 14 so much. Oh, pops, pops, my darling Popsie, I love you. With all n heart, mind and body, I love you. I adore you. I worship you my pops.

Pops, I've been hoping all day that I'd get to see you today. But so far no go. Damn, Hell, Cuss words.

I'm lonesome for you.

My sweet Popsie, will I ever get over hating to think of any other man? I don't know how you feel, but that's the way I feel. Just a great big lonesomeness in all of me. Missing all of you so dreadfully. Loving you so much. Adoring and worshipping you. Wanting m pops. All I've got is you pops, you're my whole life.
Darling, darling, please don't leave me, don't be unfaithful.

I adore you Popsie, darling, my wonderful, beautiful, gorgeous Pops, my intelligent, handsome pops.

Your loving gal
Louise

———

4-13-47   *27th day in jail*
8:30 A.M.   *42 days to trial*

My Baby dear, I love you, I adore you – I want you. All the time I want you. Geemonie Chrismiss – I thought you knew my parents better than to think they would be after your money. And, as far as I am concerned I wish you would have Mr. Jacobs draw up a paper like this.

I, George Rector Gollum, for the consideration of one dollar ($1) already received, do hereby release and absolve Miss Beulah Louise Overell, my future lawful wife of any financial responsibility to me.
Aforementioned Louise (?) Gollum to retain the complete management and title to and of all said property. Investing and reinvesting her profits and earnings thereof to her own advantage and desires provided further that they not be conferred in any way on the said George Rector Gollum, her future lawful husband.

By my hand signed and sealed this 13th day of April, 1947.

GEORGE RECTOR GOLLUM

There honey, by damn! Now do you still think I am after your money?

I just saw Kaufman. He says "He isn't sure whether we should get married right away or not." Time many conferences will tell.

Mr. Jacobs, my competitor is up in S.F. I hear. Well, well, well. Can you stand his being away? No kidding" I'm jealous. I'm sorry I did not hurt you that last time. I'll try again as soon as I get the chance.

Where should I try to leave a mark? Please answer.

Regardless of how the trial turns out, I am not going to be separated from you any longer than the end of the trial!

Of course, I don't know your uncles very well at that, but it sure seems funny to me that they don't stop to consider the fact that if I get acquitted, you are positive to get acquitted also. But, if I get a sentence you will probably be roped in only a charge of manslaughter, as an accessory before and after the fact.

Besides all of which, if you get sentenced to anything you won't have an estate. The only sentence I will take is full acquittal.

You say I shouldn't be trustful. Don't you read my letters? I told you before that I trust no one but you! Y – O – U. and YOU alone. Not even my illustrious parents.

Don't tell anyone about those Jimmy Nelson's of mine. The prosecution has not, I understand, any motive, as yet, for us. AS I see it, their whole case hinges on connecting us or me directly with the dynamite and our being the last people on-board.

It might not be customary for you to rape me but wouldn't it be fun? You could tie me down to a bed stead, take a scissors to my apparel, and wreak you desires upon me. Woo, woo! You take it from there.

New subject. I have been thinking that they might try to say I did it and you love me so much you are shielding me.

You can take my word for it, I am going to be "real masculine" when I get at you on our honeymoon, and for a long time afterwards. All our lives. I even have thought of lots of way to act. F'ristance my tying you spread-eagled and doing my will. And then I'm going to rip off your dress, and tear off your bra, and rip your panties. Then I'll beat you on the tummy and grab your breasts hard, and bruise them and make your nipples all red and swollen from feeling and biting and sucking. And I'll put my tongue in Butch, and my finger, and Junior. Then I'll F*** the hell out of you. This is all a promise my darling. A promise.

The guy I'm getting the money from is an ex-shipmate of mine who I lent money when together in the Navy. He is an "Okie" and oil has been opened up on his land. He is putting aside a certain percentage for me. Just because I let him that money.

I sure am glad that no one could talk you out of marrying me, I thought they couldn't and now you say so, why I am sure happy. If we are married in here then I want you to go straight home with me. But if we aren't married by the end of the trial, why I want you to leave with me, not more than an hour after the jury says "Not Guilty." We will then go to Nevada or Arizona and be married, stay there over night, and then come back here to get our personal property. Because your uncles don't know me, in the confusion after the verdict, They might try to get you in a car and away from me that way. But, I am going to grab you as soon as the jury says them wonderful words, and I'm going to hold tight to you. I want you to hold tight to me. and because your other relatives don't like me, I think they will try to get you away and everyone who wants to see one of us will have to see the other one also, Because I won't let you go. Then if we have to come back here to get our stuff out of the cells and our other stuff – jewelry and stuff from the desk. I will wait for you right there by the telephone. And you wait there for me too. I'll have Mom bring your wedding rings down with her and we can take ourselves off alone. Maybe we can have the lawyers get our gear – Would like my drivers license though – and we could maybe come back and get it the next day or so. If possible though, I don't want to have to come back into this hotel. Even for a second.

I think that, after matrimony, we might have to come back to L.A. to clear up the details, and to buy and outfit our trailer, get maps, and then away ----- into a 50,000 mile trip. Would that be enough for the first year? Just around the U.S.

I sure hope that we can have our Attorneys, or someone, clear up the property deal in this damn jail though. I wouldn't want to come back even to say "goodbye' to the guys. Not that day. Maybe after we have gotten married we could come back the next day? How do you feel about it? Just think, you are going to have to change your name drivers license – bank, etc. But all in all I don't think it should take more than three weeks, I hope to clear up the details. Of course after I'm married to you, and living with you, I don't care what happens as long as we are there and not you or I!

Now, by golly, I am going to ask you to do something that you might not like so much. But please to it. Please writer for me a sex story. One with you and me as the main characters, Please write it. Make it a couple pages long, or more. Hunh? Pretty please. And put in all the details. I want to see if I can give you some more sewing – the crotch type, See how sexy you can make it. Go on now, you've got a good imagination and I hope you can drown your inhibitions for a few minutes. Pretty please.

P.S. Baby dear, Junior sends you and Butch his love and says "Hold out a while longer and he'll help remove the cotton." Popsie.

I wish the medical examiner had been a woman. I do, I do, I do! Looking at the top of the first page you will find a number #A 1. I am going to number all of my notes from here on out. Please use the number when you write an answer. That way, I'll know when and which not you are answering – O.K.? I love you my dear one. I adore you my love is yours for now and eternity. There is no one else, there never will be anyone else, never. Yes my dear, I am thinking a lot about sex. But that is not only what I am thinking about. I might think of sex for fifteen or twenty minutes or wake up with my under shorts sort of dampish. But I am also thinking about you all the time. I worship and love and adore my baby every instant of the time. I do love you in the same way that you over me. And more so. Your, Baby – Popsie.

———

A 1

Hi, Pops!

I haven't got enough paper to write you a nice story, but tomorrow or the next day I'll try. Give me a black eye, please, in our next conference. Pretty pretty please. Otto hasn't come up yet. Heck I'm getting to the point where I'd give anything, almost, to get you in bed with me. Poor Butch is miserable. What I wouldn't give for Jr. attached to you of course.

I finished your blue sox and I'll try to have OA give them and purple ones to you. Ah darling Pops I wish I was frigid or something. Then I wouldn't miss Jr. so much. I miss you Pops so much. If only I were your wife. I know they'd let me keep my wedding ring on. That would be such a comfort. What's this joke you cracked on Easter when someone woke you up and said the Easter Bunny had been there and you looked in the rice and raisins and said evidently? All the girls were laughing so I went up and they told me. Listen, Dope, I love those jokes. The relatives are OK. Relax, I'm only worried about the verdict and whether I can hold out missing you so. Darling I've been trying to imagine life without you. It doesn't work. My Pops, I love you so much. I love you with all of me. I adore you. I worship you. You're my pops. Thank your family for everything. I can't tell you how much I appreciate it. Oh darling why do I love you so much. Otto has just been here. He is positive we will get off. Oh darling, my wonderful pops, I love you. Darling I think of you as a Presence that is more than a person. A Power all enduring. And I've got you. Please Pops I've got you? You've got me. Please Darling. I, Louise Overell,

hereby give into keeping of George Rector Gollum any money and property I receive in the course of my life under the two provisions namely 1 – that he is never in my life unfaithful to me in word or deed, thought excluded, and 2 – that he never leaves me. Being of harassed and miserable frame of mind, but sane and loving the aforesaid G R G only I declare the following to be a free and voluntary declaration. There now, but I hope you'll always love me. Oh my darling. Oh my pops, Popsie, darling, my beautiful, handsome intelligent pops, I adore you always eternally. I never want anything else but to be alone with you, working for you.
Yours alone, Louise

———————

 # A 2 4-14-47
My dearest Baby,

Hey, I think I dated that last little deal wrong. A 1 was on the 14th also. But earlier in the day, I forgot to ask you some more about that dyeing business. What's the score? You might answer my questions about that even before you get this, but in case you haven't please do. I was not joking about not wanting you to dye your hair. I really don't. And I was not kidding when I said "If you do dye your hair I'll shave it all off." And I mean all. Every bit of hair you own dyed or undyed head hair or body hair. If you dye any of it at all, off comes the hair and into hibernation you go until it all grows out natural.

As I said before you have no reason for wanting to dye your hair. It is a wonderful color now. Just the color I want it. If what I want means anything. That's a nasty way of trying to get your to do something, or not to do something, but sometimes drastic measures have to be taken. I hope I'll get a note from you tonight. I don't know whether you'll get this today or Wednesday. We'll see.

I love you my dear. I adore you with all my heart and soul. I miss your voice. I miss your presence, I miss you, I miss your body. My darling I do so wish you were with me right now. I wish we were in our own home alone. That's why I don't want to have a housekeeping couple living in a house of ours. We wouldn't have complete freedom. We would not be able to run around the house naked. We wouldn't be able to make <u>UN-RESERVED</u> love anywhere any time. I couldn't get a desire all of a sudden down in the front room and just rip the clothes off you right there and sooth my passion. Yu wouldn't be able to take your desires any place, anytime either. N'est-ce Pas? Those are the special reasons why I don't want to live in a big house that requires a couple until after we had been married for about umpteen years. Enough years so that we could contain ourselves until we got behind a door anyway. We are going to need very thick rugs on our floors. And furniture with no sharp edges, all smooth and comfortable angles. You are going to get it in all and every position and way possible. I understand the Special Prosecutor is going to interview us. Maybe together. I hope he does it together.

I miss you! I want and desire you. I want to just lay with your soft and warm naked body laying on top of me or by my side. Thinking, and talking and loving. On a blanket in the woods under a tree. Or in our own bed. Or on the beach at night with the waves sighing on the sand. Just you and me alone, as nature intended us to be. Alone and at peace with the world. Alone and with a wonderful feeling in our hearts. Living a life at times wild and turbulent with bared feelings and at others, calm and smooth with the soothing knowledge of perfect companionship, the satisfaction of life fulfilled. The desires of the moment expiated, and the soothing influences of our own perfect full-blown love lulling us into the calmness and peace of paradise together. To be with you every moment of the day and night. To be ever at your side. That is what I want. You will probably get very tired of having me around all the time, but there I will be anyway. You will never escape me. You cannot, and I won't let you leave me. I love you, I adore and need you, and desire and feel you with all my physical and mental powers. The real you, the all of you. Not just your physical body alone, but the sound and feeling of your voice, the smell of you, the force of your mind and your mental power, your wonderful personality and your magnificent character. My dearest I get a sensual, almost sexual, thrill every time I hear your voice, every time your beautiful mind is working. When you talk to me and discuss your ideas, I get a wonderful pleasure from it. My dearest baby doll, I adore you to pieces.

This letter, from the top of page four is being written on 4-15-47. Tuesday. I did not get a letter from you yesterday. That is because the relief matron was on. That's why you did not get a letter from me yesterday either. I understand that during the day the tank up there is open and the dames wander all around. Is it true? When you take a bath don't you have any privacy at all? Do they just stand around and watch? If so, I don't like that. Are you locked in your cell all day long or do you get out occasionally? How is your cold? And your hair? Are you going to be able to keep it or do I shave it off? Do you get clean sheets often? I am going to see if I can't get your glasses up to you. The ones in the car. And when you get them _I want you to wear them._

I sure hope I get a letter from you today. This is our 28th day since incarceration and the 41st day until the trial. It is also the 34th day since Junior swelled into Butch. _Damn it._ After we are out of here and married I ain't going to miss one day. Blood or not – unless _you_ don't want me to. _That_ will be the only reason from now on. Let's see. 12 time 365 – 4380 times the first year after marriage. O.K.? I did not hurt you last Friday, but, did it feel good? Do they bring candy bars and stuff up there for you? Or do you just get the stuff your relatives and my parents bring?

That piece of cloth I gave you was one half of a handkerchief of mine- the other half has lipstick on it. It has a G in one corner. If you want to you could keep the G. and just use the rest of the handkerchief.

Remember? You said you would to it. Put the cloth in Butch – get it entirely wet then dry it off and send it to me. you said you would. I hope you will keep your promise this story.

I am sorry you don't want me to touch the mounts or Butch. I don't know why you don't. Mr. J. and Mr. K. were not able to see my actions. Mr. J. had his back to you and Mr. K. was hidden behind him. But that is O.K. I guess. That's what _you_ want?
I know I liked to have your hand on Junior. If you really don't want me to put my hands on you, please tell me and at our next conference I won't.

I still can't help thinking that it is <u>you</u> who has been reading too many books. Please tell me if it does disturb you to have me touch you. I <u>do not</u> want to do anything that will bother you. Please tell me.

I don't know how I can reach you and hold you when you are constantly being hit, mentally, from all sides, by people who are trying to get us apart. That fortune teller might even have been put with you just for the purpose of making you mad at me, or anxious. She seems to have done a good job. Or have you retreated back into your shell with me I can see how possible it is. But only possible if you are willing to believe others instead of myself, only if you have no faith in me. I have no way to get to you. Perhaps that is the way to get to you. Perhaps that is the way it must be. This period when all we have are questions and answers and those by hidden notes and on all sides lies and falsehoods of every kind, it is perhaps a good proving ground for our love. I know and am positive that my love for you is strong and will not alter or falter while I have life. It is growing stronger each and every day and night. I have heard stories of you writing out to other boys. I have heard stores from various means, not my parents, that you are only stringing me along until the trial is over and hiding behind the statement that I am just "after your money." You are going to throw me down. I have heard these and lots of other tales – But that is what I call them, Tales. I don't believe them or place any truth in them because you write me that you love me. That is good enough for me. Your saying that you love me and are faithful to me is all I need. I will never believe anything I hear – in court – in the papers – from reliable people – unless you tell me it is so yourself. Don't you see my dearest, I love you. You can do no wrong. And no one can tell me that you are doing me dirt. I believe in you. As long as you tell me you love me and there is no one else in your heart, I am happy and contented. Even if someone showed me a picture of some other man holding you, I would not think anything of it unless you told me yourself that it meant something.

I trust and have faith in you. I expect you to trust and have faith in me. If you don't I don't think you truly love me. I could be shown proof that you were being unfaithful to me and the whole world could be crying it, but if <u>you said you were not</u>, I would not believe anyone else. Am I too trustful *of you? Should I doubt you? I don't know. All I do know is that I love you. I could not live without you. And I have faith in you.*

Please my dear don't allow what spiteful people and strangers and people motivated by hell knows what ideas, come between our love. Don't let them destroy that which we have built up. Or, if you are going to listen to them, even over my wish, at least accord me the dignity of asking me before you jump to conclusions. Today, as you started up the stairs with the matron, I noticed a tear in your eye. You had just told me that I had been with another girl on March 2. I was with no other girl on Mar 2 or any time since the eighteenth of June, when I was discharged, have I been with any other girl but you. If you believe me then I will know that you still love me. If you don't, then I will know what people have been saying is true and you never did love me. Before you had money, you personally, I don't think you ever thought I would marry you for your wealth. But now, when you do have it, why right away you start to worry and wonder if I am not just a fortune hunter. What do you want? Do you want to postpone our marriage until I have enough money to support you in "the fashion to which you are accustomed?" Are you trying to brush me off? What is it? Don't you still want to marry me? Or do you want to wait "Until I have made something of myself?" That is what your relatives want I am sure. Have they talked you into it too?

So "Everybody" says you have lost me? Is that what they say, or do they all say "I have lost you?"

Have they taught you into confusion and doubt? Here in a place where everything is lies and subterfuge and falsehood and mental confusion have they, whoever "they" are, succeeded in making our love look false and bad in your eyes and mind? Are these your own ideas? My wanting you for your money? I am all confused I guess. I can't seem to figure out if these doubts you have are from your own mind or what people have told you. And that fortune teller. Your believing her. And "She has never been wrong." Well, this guy down here has "never been wrong" either. So what's the deal? All I can ask is that you have faith in me. Regardless of what people say. Regardless of what is said at the trial. Have faith, remember our love, and trusting. I can ask no more. I don't see how you can grant me less. I don't think I have ever given your cause mis-trust. Have I?

I guess I must admit that your hair does look becoming, the color it is now. I think it would have been nice before that Mr. J. suggested it. He did suggest it did not he?

You said today that your seat is getting sore from sitting around all day doing your needle work and knitting and all. For once I would prefer that you write for me rather than to knit for me. Unless it is for someone else of course.

This will be my last <u>long</u> letter for a while I guess. I write 16 pages or 14 pages and get 1 or 2 in reply. The percentage is against me, or maybe I am not worth more effort. Besides which you never answer the questions I ask. Or do the things I ask. Or believe what I write about either. You tell me. Do you want me to continue writing long letters? Or do you want me to write short letters? Do you really care? Or does the fact that you don't think I am being faithful, and not answering my questions and not doing what I ask you to do in your letters to me – and not telling me about your hair – mean that you <u>don't</u> care? I hope not my dear. I hope that every-thing is as before. I hope that you are not changing in relation to our love for each other. I hope that your love for me is as strong as my love and faith and trust are for you. I hope that you will develop your faith and trust in me as mine is in you.

With the, perhaps, good news we were told today, it would appear that our chances of acquittal are increasing daily. If I don't have your love and faith and trust after we are acquitted, if by then you have decided that you had enough of me, then there would be no use of my being <u>acquitted.</u> If you ever leave me I will die. If you are ever unfaithful, <u>He</u> will die. You will never lose me. You will never get loose from me. Let the people talk. Let the trifling old fortune teller vend her lies. You will never get a pro-posal of marriage from anyone else unless I am dead.

I see you have been thinking about the things, some of them anyway that I wrote. I am afraid that you might get away too, or be gotten away in some manner. Don't you see, after the trial, your guardians could force you to get into an auto and whisk you away to a place where I could not find you for many months. I don't want that to happen, don't you see? I don't even want to let go of your hand or your arms for a second after our acquittal until we are married.

It isn't unreasonable for me to presume that you yourself aren't sure I am not marring you for your money. Your relatives might even be less sure and want you away from me until you have forgotten me or gotten interested in someone else and married to him. And this might be done by fair means or foul. I repeat what I said once before. I trust no one but you. NO ONE – bar nobody – I trust you and you alone. And here you don't even trust me. I guess you must trust someone else. Who? Mr. J.? I don't trust him or Mr. K. either. Not completely. Oh baby, I love you, I love you, I adore you. Don't ever leave me, don't let anyone tell you that you have lost me because that is not true. You have me more than ever. I am yours in any way you want me.

I think that your getting all that money is, in a way, too damn bad. Before you had it you weren't worried about me marrying you for your money. And now you are worried about just that. By damn – be damned to your money. Give it away. Give it to some charity or something. I want you and I want you without doubt. You are going to have to trust me. I won't ever let you go.

That's all there is to it I won't ever let you go regardless whether you love me or not – damn your relatives and that fortune teller, and the matrons and Mr. J. Damn the whole kit and caboodle of them. I am going to marry you. You are going to marry me even if you don't love me. You can even scream and kick and beat at me and curse me and anything else. I have made up my mind that you want me to be one of those "iron fists in a velvet glove" deals. O.K. Iron it is. Just watch out the glove doesn't come off and the fist bruise your tender skin. I just counted your notes. There have been ten of them - ten notes, ten pieces of paper. There are going to be ten pieces of paper in this note – it came to 13. That's about ten to one, isn't it. Now I wonder who loves who the most? I wonder who misses who the most? I wonder who writes to who the most? I wonder who has the most reason to doubt the faith of who? And yet I wonder who it is who does the doubting?

I guess it isn't doing either of us any good to be irritated at each other all the time.

———

I want to say again, pardon me for putting my hands on your breast today and trying to put my finger in Butch. If you had told me that you did not want me to, in a letter – you knew from mine I was going to try – Or right there asked me not to, I wouldn't have tried. I still thought everything was the same as before. I know I liked your hand on Junior. You missed the scratches too. No soap. I would like you to put your hand on Junior next Wed. If it doesn't bother you. Maybe I'm being unfair. Maybe there was a good reason why you did not want me to touch your breasts or Butch. Is there? Was there a special reason? Please tell me if there was.

Do you mind if I talk about your body? If you don't want me to, I won't but it makes me feel good to talk about the parts of your body. For instance I have been thinking about your breasts, both of them. They are beautiful, both of them. Proud and out thrust and pink tipped. I like them even better when you have your shoulders back. Maybe it will make you even more self-conscious. But I think I have mentioned it before. I think you should hold your shoulders back. It gives your better freedom in breathing and it doesn't crush the organs in your chest. Not only do they look better but is better for them. No kidding. It really is better for you to hold your chest up. See how far out you can thrust your chest and how far back you can pull your shoulders. And if you have a mirror, or are able to see your silhouette against a wall, notice how much nicer your posture is. Your breast will be in the prominence yes, but gee, you are a woman. And are expected to have breasts N'est-ce pas? And as you do have them and very good looking and well shaped, and well placed, why not be proud of *them instead of trying to hide them? I know I am proud of your breasts. I am very proud of them. Even if it makes you embarrassed for me to write about them. That's one of the reasons I like to put my hands on them. I know that all your life you have been taught that the body is something that should not be talked about. But just you wait – I'm going not only to talk about your body, I am going to make you use it to its best advantage. Your whole body is beautiful, lovely, and I am going to make you as conscious as I can of the fact that with me at least you are going to hold your shoulders back. And I'm going to be with you always so you'd better practice,. I am going to buy you special bras too, $30 or $40 apiece so that you will have the best support for your breasts as it is possible to get. That'll be my money by the way, not yours. Inside of our house tho, if you'll agree we'll be without clothes most of the time. I think nudity is healthful. <u>What do you think about that?</u> You will have a great deal of support for your breasts most of the time and I don't mean brassieres either. I mean my hands. Do I hear any objections?*

I also like your breasts when you are lying on your back. They are nice and soft. And when the nipples are a little excited they stand up so perkily. And your nipples have such a beautiful red rose color when they have been sucked on. And when I am laying down and you are leaning over me naked I love the way your breasts look then. They are so beautiful. And I like to feel them so much and I look to have you put your nipples in my mouth. OH GEE HONEY, I'll stop talking about them now. I don't want you to get mad. But I do wish you were here with me now naked and with Junior throbbing in Butch, and my hands on your proud beautiful breasts, and I wish I was French Kissing you. I wish, I wish, I wish. Oh God I wish that we were free right now and that we were man and wife. Right this minute. This second. Even through all this tirade I know that we will be married and live the rest of our lives happily after we are acquitted. I know because I know how much I love you. I know that my love for you is growing larger and greater and stronger with each passing second. I love you and want you. No one but you. Nothing but you. No money – no clothes, no cars, no house, if we could just go out in the woods naked and alone I think we would be the happiest of anyone alive today.

Out where we had to make our own clothes – shelter, catch our food and everything we had or ate was the result of our efforts.

I guess I'm just a primitive at heart. I don't care how we live or where, as long as I'm with you. That's all I want, to be with you. Just you and me in a trailer. For quite a few months. Then we can settle down or do some more traveling or whatever <u>we</u> want to do. I am sure beginning to hate the word <u>money</u>. And I mean <u>hate.</u> Every where I turn now it is money! Money! You aren't the only one who keeps telling me I am trying to marry you for your money – Jack – moola –berries – call it what you will. They all mean the same thing.

In case you forgot so soon, I'll tell you once more about the deal where we are going to get a lot of dough.

When I was in the Navy I lent a guy $600. Another guy lent this guy a like amount. He had to go home to Okla. for some reason. He has since been discharged and so forth. Returning home he found he had oil on his land. The man next to him had a smaller piece of property and was bought out for 10 million. This guy is now thinking of selling and after all taxes have been taken out he will clear over 10 million himself. Well, he has been splitting his profits into thirds. One third for him one third for the other guy who lent him $600 and one third for me – us that is. So you see. When he sells, or even now we have a sizable chunk of dough even without your personal cash. Now will you please stop telling me I'm marrying your for your money?
I love you my honey darling. So long, Louise, with all my love forever –
Bud Popsie

–––––

Hi, Popsie;

Guten morgen. Comment allez vous? Wie gehst du? As soon as we are acquitted I will meet you at the telephone down stairs. I <u>promise</u> you that <u>nothing</u> will move me until you come along. Pops I am out of my cell from 7 AM to 9PM. Unfortunately, since I'm such a dangerous character, I have to have someone see I don't fall down the drain while I take a bath. We can wash our sheets whenever we feel like it. Do you have mattresses? The day matron taught me how to play cribbage. I got my glasses a long time ago and I gave them to Marjorie to get different rims for me. My inspiration for Spanish being downstairs I don't study much but if you want me to I will. Sure we get candy bars if we want them. Don't eat too many. I can't think of any good story darling, you write one then maybe I'll do one. I'm rather busy all day so I don't have too much time to write. Did you get your knitting? You'd better. Please, Pops, get started doing something. I don't know what your arrangement is down there, but please keep busy. Darling, my sweet wonderful pops, I adore you. I'm so afraid you won't or don't love me and will leave me. Darling if that ever happens I'll take an overdose of sleeping pills. Warning! I've got to go enlarge coffee can covers. Oh darling! Oh Pops! I love you so much. I think you've been reading too many books. I just got a sack containing three cup cakes for "Bud George Gollum." So sorry, Pops, but I've eaten them. Oh Pops I love you so much I could eat you. Darling, don't forget me. Don't stop loving me. You aren't smoking are you? I sort of hope you're not, but if you are, do you enjoy it? I can't but even if I could, I wouldn't because you don't want me to.

What happens if I get acquitted and you don't? Where will I go to wait and what will I do? Sometime full details pliz, pops. I've been so busy all day. It's 3:00 now and I haven't been still three minutes. First the coffee can covers, then enlarging the cook's pants and patching them. Then the machine stuck, due to too much stuck thread. Oh Popsie, I've missed you so much All of me misses you all the time. Just received beautiful package from your parents. Thank them but please, no more yarn for a while. I've got needle point to embroider 4 ½ pairs of sox, and a sweater. I'm so busy I almost can't go to sleep. And I have millions of tomatoes to eat. Gosh! Pops I love you. If it helps any, never think I won't love you, always remember that I love you, that all my affection is centered upon you, now and forever. Does it help to know that you're the only person who means anything to me and you mean everything to me? Nothing I do is without thinking of you in some connection with it. Every thing I do makes me better and more worthy to be your wife. Darling, that will be my future, *you wiling. I promise you that I will devote all my time and efforts in making you happy and satisfied. This separation makes me realize How truly wonderful you are, and makes me feel, again, that I am not good enough for you, My darling Pops, how did I ever get you? I can't believe that I have such a man. Do I really have you? You know don't you, that you have me? Popsie I miss you so much I'm so lonely and miserable without you. I don't know what else to write. You write such beautiful letters and they say exactly how I feel toward you, that when it comes to writing to you, I could only copy one of yours. I'm worried. If we don't get some one new in before tomorrow morning I'm going to be the only white girl in here. There will be four Mexicans one of which speaks English. Happy days. Tell your family how much I enjoy their contributions to my welfare. I love you, I adore you, I dream of you every night and quite a few nights I'm getting you into a compromising situation in which Jr. play an obvious part. Oh Pops never leave me, please please never leave me Never love anyone else I love you so tremendously. Those damn men! They just brought a lot of mending. Damn, Damn! What heat is on? Darling, what are they doing to you? What's happening? Don't let them worry you. Please, Pops, everything will be all right. What heat? I sure wish you were in bed with me this second and many millions of seconds to come. I got the joke, dear, I'm really not too stupid. Well you've got me for always. I love you so much. I wish you were here so I could play with Jr. and try to tickle you and love you. What heat, pops, is something wrong? I'll try to give you the sox as soon as possible. I love you, I adore you. You're my life. You're what I live for. You and Jr. are the only things I live for.*

Yours always, Louise.

Friday A 4 – 4-18-47
31 days in jail
38 days till trial

My Baby Darling,
Damn Mr. Jacobs to <u>*hell*</u>*. O.K. so he is your lawyer, so you think he is a swell, man. So he's my competitor. I thought the four of us had an understanding that we would have a conference today. And why don't we? I'll tell the world why, "The illustrious Mr. Jacobs is in Los Angeles." That's why. And I am pissed off. He might have had to go. It might have been*

something really important. But damn it, he could have at least told Mr. Kaufman that he was going. He could have let Mr. K. know that there was no conference today. All week I dream of this day. I lied there on my bunk and dream of seeing you. Of holding you in my arms, of kissing you. I dream of hearing your voice, of burying my face in your hair, of smelling the wonderful sweet smell of you. I dream and imagine that you are looking into my eyes. Of telling you how much I love you. I dream of holding your breast in my hands and squeezing. I dream, if the turn their heads for a minute or two, of putting my hand on your leg and sliding it under your dress, and putting my finger in Butch and wiggling my finger. I dream of bruising you, perhaps Butch, maybe your leg. Maybe your lovely, smooth, enticing breast. A bruise that would last for a few days to remind you of me. I dream of having a bruise that will remind me of you. A bruise that I can push and have it hurt. A wonderful pleasurable hurt that will remind me of you, that will bring you into the circle of my arms.

My dearest sweet one, I miss you so terribly. I so wanted to see you. I wanted you to put your hand on Jr. I wanted you to kiss me hard. I wanted you to kiss me so hard it bruised my lips. Oh, gee! Honey lamb, I so wanted to see you. I hope you knew ahead of time that you weren't to see me and did not spend the morning and noon time thinking about it only to get a terrible disappointment. I can't take many deals like that. I got up this morning and shaved real close you couldn't feel it at all, and took a long shower and put on a clean "t" shirt, and those blue rayon shorts you got me and those red sox. And just wandered around waiting for the guard to come and call me. And then he did, but it was only the doctor who wanted to take a blood specimen. I did not let him have it, and then back I came and then 10:20 soup, and still no call. The vegetables came in around 11:00, that's when the call came last Friday, but still no call. Then at 1:00 (13:00) the call came, and I went out with a big grin spattered all over my face and here was Mr. Kaufman and we went into that little room and sat down and then he let me have it. "No Visit." And then he told me why. "Mr. Jacobs is in Los Angeles today." And Mr. K. can't get you out, and Mr. J. can't get me out so there we were, stuck. OH DAMN! I was counting on seeing you today. I was depending on it. I was dreaming and thinking about it. I love you so much. I want you so much.

Mr. K said that he would try and get a conference for sometime around the first of next week. O gee, I hope so. Monday I hope, I hope, I hope!

I love you, I love you, I love you. I am yours darling. If after this is all over, you are still willing to have me I am yours. That is a misleading sentence. Because you are mine and you aren't going to get away from me. I am going to have you as my wife. Because I love and worship you and cherish you with all my heart. With every bit of me I love every bit of you. And whether you love me and want me or not, when this is over, you aren't going to be able to get rid of me. Even if you don't want me, I am selfish enough to take you. And keep you. If necessary, I'll kidnap you and carry you off somewhere so that no one will ever be able to find us and there I'll make passionate and violent love to you. Ripping and tearing and beating you. And ripping and tearing your clothes from you. And taking my lust and desires out on you. I will rip your dress off of you, and then put my hand on your brassiere straps and break them, and then I'll grab your brassiere in front. There where that magnificent valley runs down between your soft exquisite beast and jerk it so that it will break the straps in back where it is hooked, exposing your beautiful white mounds of pink tipped breasts, in all their beauty and glory. I'll make you bend over me and place your nipples in my mouth and while I am sucking and biting on one of them I'll tickle the other one and run my tongue over their naked loveliness. Then I'll grab your panties and rip them off of your most wonderfully shaped hips exposing Butch in his forest hidden mystery and ecstasy, and joy and desire. I'll run my hands over your virgin, except for me, hips and down your shapely buttocks, pinching and gouging at you. And I'll lay down on the floor with you on top of me and my head between your legs and I'll put my tongue in Butch and work my fingers around on Butch, and in front of him, remember that real ticklish place? And back and have my tongue deep in Butch and my fingers deep in another place. And I'll excite you a lot. Then a wriggle and you on the bottom and me on top with me stretched down between your legs and my face and tongue still in Butch and then a slow progress up your body, with my tongue leaving the whole area of your stomach and Butch's hair all wet and a little pool in your navel and a wet trail up to one of your breasts and the sucking and biting, and from one swollen, throbbing pink nipple a wet trail across to the other beautiful redwork of nature. A similar treatment to that nipple and two swollen, red, surging pools of desire make known their positions. Up your chest, to your neck, in your ear, a hot breath a pant and a bite on your ear lobe. Down your neck across to the other ear, again a rush of air and panting breath, a bite of burning desire then across your wonderful chin to your full parted lips a gasp of breath, and I'll kiss you as I've never kissed you before. A long lasting promise of future love. A sweet flow of your saliva into my mouth as I French kiss you, with my tongue tickling, a moment of hesitation, a fumbling around the outside of Butch and a sudden thrust! And Junior pulsing and throbbing, jams his way with an outrush of desire into the innermost recesses of Butch. Panting and sweating, with your legs locked behind and straining against mine, minutes of pleasure and a primitive feeling, until, with a sudden stiffening of Junior, a flood of hot, steaming juice flows in you from me. A silence, a few minutes of rest, panting, breath catching, and then a time of recuperation. After several minutes, I reach over and grab your breast in my hand Tenderly, gently, I caress it. I softly titillate your tender, oh so tender, nipple, then a sudden violet shaking. Did you like it when I did that? Or did it hurt? Remember? I held your breast and wiggled it quickly back and forth. What did it feel like? A further diddling. I put my fingers again down into Butch. No towel was used the first time. The triple covering on the bed will protect it? Gently and then firmly I move my fingers around. I put my face down on to Butch, and suck hard, letting a sweet tricle of the nectar of Gods flow into my mouth. Then once more, into full bloom goes Junior Harder and harder he gets, a period of violent love making and then once more a sudden thrust as Junior again moves into his own paradise, and helps me into mine. There, now you know what is in store for you. Want to change any part of it? Does it read O.K.?

Do you want it to happen like this? Let me know please. I love you ALWAYS.

I hope that Mr. Kaufman and Mr. Jacobs get together sometime in the first of the week, I still hope Monday, for our conference. I am still of the idea that I should try to hurt somewhere where it won't show. I want it

41

to be our hurt, and not just everybody's hurt to stare at. On you Breast Beautiful Breast, Or on, on in Butch or on your leg? Please suggest a place, not really visible

And please love me, my dearest one. Love me as much as I love you. Love me with sex as a motive. Love me with my voice and body as a motive, love me with my personality and my character as a motive, and love with me as a motive. Please my darling. Love me as much and as often all the time and as completely as I do you. Is there something you want me to do for you? Walk off a cliff? Thru fire? Kill a lion? Shoot myself? Anything? For you I would maim and torture myself. I would live and try to make you happy. I wound and <u>will</u> do whatever you want me to do. Snap your whip oh mistress mine, I will obey.

Will you please do something for me? In a sex way? Take a piece of cloth several inches and <u>put it in Butch until it is completely wet.</u> Then dry it off, without washing it, and send it to me or if it is a big one, I hope, bring it to a conference with you, as a handkerchief, and give it to me. <u>Please do this</u>. I will taste it and let Junior feel it, and keep it with me. Please do this for me. Junior wants you to do it too. He won't be jealous of the piece of cloth.

By the way Dear Otto is still on my personal black list. And I don't like the fact that you like him so much either. I'm jealous. Honest I am. I feel just like you did after the Rick's incident.

—————

My darling baby doll I love you with all of me. I love and adore you. I love and want, and need, and adore, and desire <u>y o u.</u> And regardless of what you say or anyone says I AM going to marry you, and have children by you and with you, and cherish you, and put you in sexual passions, and bring out your desires and so-called baser emotions,. Whoever said that must have been a frigid old prude. Baser emotions <u>Hell!</u> Those emotions called baser by some are in reality the most wonderful and most complex of them all. They are truly beautiful. That is what I really think and believe. I think the emotions and acts of <u>sex</u> are the most beautiful and necessary of any possessed by human beings. In the word sex I include all the thoughts I have about you. My love is sex. My desire to protect you is sex. My thrilling to the sound of your voice is sex. No, I, not a disciple of Freud. You know how much of him I've read. Nill – I just truly think that all the emotions and feeling between two people – between us – is sexual. But sexual in a way that is good, and healthy, and will as the years pass strengthen our lives together. My dear one, My baby, my doll, I love you and refuse to let you go either now or ever. I am going to bind you to me with binding stronger than chains, with the strongest ties I know, with my love for you and your love for me. <u>I love you.</u>

I asked Mr. Lord – as a good guy – one of the guards, for those pictures of you I had in my wallet, remember? They were gone, along with the picture of my real old-man. The picture of you that was in the glove compartment of the car is also missing. I hope I find out who has them. They'll really have something to pin on me. That's twice today I've been peed off. Once about the conference, and now about the pictures. I did really want them. I'll tell Kaufman that they are gone and see if I can't have him take the rest of my property away. How about all of those notes I wrote you that were in that little brow inner-pocket book in your purse? Are they still around? Better not ask Jacobs until we see each other next week.. They might think it is funny if we both brought out the idea at the same time. There is a bit of heat on the <u>note writing</u> right now. Someone is a stooly or one of us made a slip. I could have, or one of the guys here saw a note coming in. There are all kinds of possibilities. I sure hope we don't have to discontinue writing though. Hay! – I love you. Yesses I love you. Vous este a <u>femme,</u> vous este ma espouses. Vous este ma cher. Dear baby, I just got your reply to my last two notes. The heat deal is about these notes The guard who is carrying them is being and has been asked if he was carrying them. So I won't be able to write for a while. I don't even know if I can take these right off. Maybe in a few days.

I wrote a sort of story in this letter. You could write a better one than that. Why not try. C'mon now, let's see what you can do. Please! I'll even send some more paper.

Why don't you answer my question about your hair? What is the score? Did you have it dyed anyway? Well, O.K. But why not tell me about it even so? Don't keep me in suspense all the time. Let me know what goes. Please! Please!

About the stuff that is on the top of page 13. They might find something in that they could use in their prosecution. So I would like Mr. Jacobs to get them and hold them if possible. See?

I'll tell the folks about the yarn. I haven't gotten anything on knitting yet. But I'm trying. No, I'm not smoking and have no intentions of doing it. I'm glad that you aren't smoking either. Please don't ever.

My dearest, I love you so much. I wish so much that you and I were in bed together right now. We've so any wonderful memories about certain things. I've so darn many wonderful memories of the peace and content- ment and joys and passions and desire that we shared on and between the same sheets as we lay tight together, intermingled in our nakedness. Darling how I long for the sweet warmth of your naked body against my naked body.

–––––

A 4 -4 - 19 – 47 32 D.I.J
37 D.T.T
Dearest Baby Doll I love you.
*   Just saw the parents – I don't have knitting needles and stuff, shucks. Notes temporarily stopped for precaution.*

I love you – Please what has been done to your hair? Anything? Noth- ing? Is it dyed? Is it cut? Please tell me. I sent the three cup cakes up. Your name was on the other side. I sure hope you and I will get together for a conference. SOMETIME DAMN SOON. I hope, I hope. I sure love you to pieces, Regardless of how we have to go, I am going to marry you. I am going to love you from now on. There will never be anyone else, only you.

Hurray – just got told that the notes are O.K. Write a story – something like the one in this only longer.

—————

Sunday
Hello pops darling,

I'm still working hard on <u>our</u> Hope Chest. Would you still marry me if I were broke? Oh pops darling <u>please promise</u> you'll marry me.. Please, pops, and stick to your promise. Please marry me Popsie, please, And stay with me.

I <u>know</u> that we will be acquitted. Believe that.

Please marry me and don't leave me pop, I miss you so much. I love you so much. I adore you. Oh pops I love you. I get to see you tomorrow at 10:30. Hooray, Oh pops please promise. I don't want anything else but you, and I am so afraid I'll lose you.

Darling if you should ever marry anyone else, I think that would be the worst thing that could ever happen to me. I hereby resolve to follow you wherever you go and prevent in any possible way, an intimate contact with another woman. Pops I can't lose you. Everyone tells me I have lost you. Oh pops please don't be lost.

My gosh! Just got A4 and have you been reading books! I have been very blue all day but I started laughing so hard at reading your desires that I feel a lot better. Don't be insulted. We've got a whining character up here and I've told her off. Hah, we aren't speaking. Pops, you're a guiding spirit. Whenever I do anything I consult with you to find out if you'd approve. My idea of you I consult with, that is.

As to my desires – 1st I want to sit and look at you, then I want to sit and unbutton your shirt, and play in your forest. Then I'll undo your belt buckle, and the gamos on your pants, and slide them off over yourselves, which I will now have to stop and undo. So now here you are in your shorts. So I'll now tickle your ankles. Oh pops, I miss you so much. I'm so *afraid I'll never marry you. I'm afraid to leave you after we're acquitted. I'm afraid to go get my stuff, because you might get, or be gotten away. Pops, pops, oh pops. Well, anyway, after tickling your ankles I stand up close to you and rub against Jr. Then I'll remove, quite hastily, your shorts, and making you lie down quite heavily on me Jr. shall be put into Butch, and with my legs fastened behind yours why we will spend the next few minutes in long anticipated pleasure.*

Pops, I can't explain how I feel about you. It is sufficient to say that you are my whole and only interest in life, that you are my rock, the thing I want when I am hurt, or sick or sad or happy, Popsie, I cannot lose you without losing myself. I cannot forget you. You are too important to me. NEVER LEAVE ME NEVER STOP LOVING ME.

Darling, that's so much to ask yet I ask it of you because I love you so much, depend on your so terribly. I'm not much good at letter writing. I'll try to scratch you at our next conference,

Your ever loving Louise

_____

A 5 4-20-47 33 D.I.J.
36 D.T.T.
My Beloved Baby Doll;
You know what I've been laying here dreaming about? You! What a wonderful thought you are. Just the pure and simple thought of you is love, pure and simple love. I just got your note. So Otto says you won't want to marry me after the trial. H E L L. You'd better want to marry me. You can talk to your heart's desire now I will never believe that your relatives are not telling him to try and separate us. I am of the opinion more than ever now. It makes be so God damn mad! Here I am where I can't talk to you, and you don't believe what I write in these letter, you still think I'm after your money don't you. And those damn relatives keep harping at you. Themselves, and Otto Jacobs too. Will you please stop calling him Otto? I beg of you, please! Call him Mr. Jacobs, at least when you write to me. Evidently you don't think I can be jealous, or possessive. Well I can be and am. I get so God damn mad when you pay no attention

to what I say. I'm sure going to rake your panties down, and hike your dress up, and spank your pretty little Buttocks! So, and so again, you can tell Mr. Jacobs for me that I think he is a <u>bastard</u>. I'm not just kidding.

If I think, at any time from now till the trials end, that you are beginning not to love me, or losing faith in me, <u>I will cause the wheels to be set in motion for our leaving</u>. You'd better read that again and remember it.

What's the matter anyway? I ask you to do things in letters and ask questions in letters sand you don't do them and don't answer the questions. Why? Will you please tell me why? No, I haven't gotten into any more fights and I'm not likely to. You can blame my not seeing you and your not seeing me on your <u>lovable Mr. Jacobs</u>. He evidently can't remember from one Friday to the next.

You shouldn't wonder if you will ever <u>get over hating to think of any other men.</u> You just better pray good and long and loud that you NEVER stop hating to think of other men. Cause if you do, then it is you who will have to worry about me being unfaithful. As long as you continue to love me, and are never unfaithful to me, I will never be unfaithful to you, in thought, or word or deed but just step out of line <u>once</u>. You will get beaten and bruised and perhaps even worse and then I'll lock you up in the house and you will never go anywhere, or see anyone unless you are attached to me. So be careful, be mighty careful.

Maybe you think it is a big joke to me having you remind me of your money all the time. Hell! I don't like it very well. We're not going to use it either. Instead of using your letter space to say things like that, why don't you write that story I asked for? Why don't you tell me what the score is about your hair? I'm going to stop asking about it pretty soon. I'll just figure you don't care if I know or not and nuts to me. Well I'd rather have you come right and tell me to go to hell than have you not write about what I ask. You don't even put SWAK on your envelopes any more. Maybe I've put things in this letter that I'll be sorry for when I read it over, maybe you will misunderstand them, maybe you won't answer the questions. I don't know. All I know is that I love you. With all my heart and soul I love and adore you, I want you, I want to hold you in my arms, I want you to lay there and not say a word, either of us, just lay. I want you mentally, physically and sexually. I want you and to have children by you. I love you. You ask me if I think you should go out on bail. *That is up to you.* I'm just selfish enough to tell you that I don't want you to go out on bail.

If you went out on bail you would be with your relatives all the time. They would continue to try and talk you out of loving me or marrying me. You are right that you wouldn't get to see me or write to me. You would though, have a decent bed, good food, be able to do what you wanted to do. You would undoubtedly find some young man whom you could think of without hating and whom you wouldn't think was after your money. If you want to, get yourself bailed out. I don't want you to though. I like to see you. I like to get notes from you. Strangely enough I just happen to love you. Maybe that doesn't bother you. Your notes don't seem to care. As I've already said you don't answer my questions or tell me what I ask or write stories for me, even one, even a little short one.

Maybe you are just asking me to say I don't love you so that you can feel free to do as your relatives ask. *Well, I'm not going to do that.*

I love you. Maybe if I could see you I could tell you how much. I will never tell you I don't love you, because that would be a lie and I've never lied to you. And I refuse to do so now. I love you. I am going to marry you. You are going to marry me. If you ever marry another person I will kill him. You can take your damn money and throw it to the dogs. We will have more than that for our own. No bank attached either. As I write this there are tears of self-righteousness and tears of self-pity in my eyes.

I am scared that you will think I am trying to brush you off. At the same time, I wonder if you are trying to give me a brushing. If only I could see you and hold you.

You never refer to parts of your body, or parts of mine, in your letters. Why? Can't you seem to force yourself to do it? Or do I have to be there *when you do? Or What? I seem to be able to write about them. I write about your body, your face, and eyes, and ears, and nose, and hair, and mouth and French kissing. I write about your shoulders and beautiful breasts. I write about holding your breasts in my hands, and tickling your sensitive, pink nipples. I write about holding your breasts in my mouth and sucking on them. You said at the time you liked it. Remember what you asked me to do to them? I write about how I bit your tender nipples and you squealed a little from pleasure and pain. I write about liking the skin on your and putting my tongue in your navel. I write about wetting Butch's hair with my tongue and putting my head between your legs and putting my tongue in Butch. You never did tell me how that felt. I write about having my tongue in Butch and my finger in that hole you have behind Butch. I write about having my tongue in the hole behind Butch and my finger in Butch. I write about that really sensitive little spot in front of Butch. I write about my tongue licking the inside of your legs and your thighs and your Buttocks. I write about holding your breasts in my hands, French Kissing you and forcing Junior into Butch. And your legs are pulling you tight up against me and the gush of hot fluid. I write all of this because I think it will give you pleasure to read that I remember the things I have done to you in a physical way. I ask you to write the same kind of things to me. Only about what you do to me and what you like me to do to you. Any reply? None. You write me not a line. Why? Does seeing it in writing make it seem bad to you? Has Yvonne been making any more of her insinuations? If you don't want to write about it, let me know. If you want me to stop writing about these wonderful and sacred memories let me know, please! If I am writing things that you don't like, tell me about it. Because if there is one thing I don't want to do, it's to make you <u>unhappy.</u>*

You have told me that reading letters from me makes you happy. So I write. You have told me that marriage between us is the one thing that will make your life happy for you. I have told you that the way to happiness for us lies thru marriage to you. I believe you and expect and demand that <u>you believe me.</u> I love you, I love you, I love you. As I have said before. If I even so much as think, from letter or word, that your love for me is faltering, or turning towards someone else, we will leave *them, even if I have to forcibly kidnap you. Now perhaps a word or two of explanation is in order.*

I have been in a grouch ever since I did not see you on Friday. And not being able to take it out on anyone else, I am taking it out and have been taking it out on you. You being defenseless to stop me. I am sorry that I cussed and swore. But on the whole it all amounts to this: A – I love you and am going to marry you. B – I am sure that your relatives are trying to get Mr. Jacobs to break us apart, along with them your uncle included. C – I refuse to break away from you and if I think you are trying to leave, I will kidnap you. D – I want you to tell me about your hair. I presume it is cut and dyed, but how short and what color. E – Write me a so called "Fuck" sexy story with you and me as the characters, a long and detailed one. F – above all, remember I love and am going to marry you, and that I will never be unfaithful to you, if you are ever unfaithful to me I will beat you fearfully and lock you away. From everybody but me. G – Please do what I asked you to with that piece of cloth and Butch.

My baby, I love you with all my heart. Yes, I am thinking a lot about sex. And writing about it too. But not over much. I think mostly of our memories and those things we have done together, and like so well. I remember about playing pool over at Catalina and you winning and what a good chaperson Pete was and playing Monopoly ******* Memories are all that has saved me from going insane down here – memories of our relations since the 4ᵗʰ of July, and the two conferences we have had and these notes of yours. Even if you don't answer my questions and write stories, a story – said he with a little smile, chuckle chuckle! Oh my darling, If I could only tell you how much I love you,

You said that if I was unfaithful to you you would take an overdose of sleeping pills. You need never worry about having to do that. I will never be unfaithful to you. And I am promising you now, by means of this letter, that if you ever leave me or are unfaithful to me or stop loving me I will take that overdose of sleeping pills. After I kill the man you turn to from me. That is a promise. My life is in your hands. That is not just an irrational thought by an upset mind, either. Yes my mind, what I have of one, is upset. Upset because I did not see you Friday. I still think it was because Mr. Jacobs is doing your relatives dirty work. But enough of that. I will try to stop talking about your relatives.

Monday, when you get this I think will be our 34th day apart and 35 days until the trial. Almost halfway my dearest. I will tell you a phone number to call in case you are acquitted and I am not, in a few days,

I'm going to need some dental work done when we are free again. I miss and long for you my dear. I hope and pray that I will see you before this week is too old. I want to see you and I want to hold you tight. I can't ever seem to be able to put down on paper what I want to say. I can't find the words. I'm just going to have to ask you to remember what I told you when were alone together. When we were alone in your room on Manhattan. When we were alone in my room on Carmona. When we were alone in my car. When we were alone at Flintridge. Oh gee my dearest darling Louise. I love you my sweetheart. I love and adore and miss and desire and want you.

We will be acquitted m darling. I hope we will be. I hope against hope that we will be found "<u>not</u> – <u>guilty,</u>" with all my heart and all my love for you and yours for me, I hope the jury finds us <u>not guilty.</u> If otherwise, you know what will happen.

P.S. Do you need some paper and pencil and envelopes?
Your loving guy, Bud.

———

Dearest Pops:
    You know something? I love you. Yes I adore you. Don't start edging for the door. My mind is made up. Excepting the proverbial other woman, I am out for you. I shall track you any where you go, including the mortuary. You see, young man, I'm obstinate. I'm determined. I've resolved to have you come hell or high water, even both at once. And being as positive as I am about our acquittal, I'm planning the trap. How to trap you

into honoring and not obeying until? do us part. You see, old chap, old chap, you're not an ordinary sort of man. Time out while I tell you an incidental. Remember I told you I told this girl off? Well she was just now playing checkers with another girl and made a bad play, so she said "I've just got half a mind on this game." So brilliant me says, sarcastically, "Oh, giving it your full attention." So now we're speaking less than ever. We ignore each other. That is, she ignores me and I make fun of her. More joy and happiness. You're an uplifted human being. No joke. You're the most intelligent person I've ever heard of. Einstein was a moron compared to you. You're so sensible and ever present. All-knowing etc. And handsome, beautiful, magnificent gorgeous. Yesss, you're the object of my adoration and the creature of my determination.

Monday morning; We had a busy night last night. Drunks. More fun. I'm so sleepy. But there isn't any time to go to sleep. I hope I see you soon. I love you. Well, so I brush my teeth furiously, take a good bath, brush my hair real well, and wait all excited and happy because I'm going to get to see you. So what happens? At 10:45 Dear Otto comes in and says he is making a hurried trip to L.A. Well tomorrow now. I even put on stockings. Oh damn. But I happen to know that it really is an urgent trip. Dearest Otto is making gains but I still want to see you.

Hello Popsie darling, it is Monday evening now. I've finished the napkins. We're got a woman who has been alternatingly sick and coughing since Saturday night. Gad! Popsie sweet, I love you so much. I'd give almost anything to be your wife now. To be able to use your name. If only I was L.O.G! If I were your wife, it would be so wonderful. I would really and legally be a part of you. Now there is no connection between us, we're just separate individuals, now and I want so much to be a part of you. I want so much to marry you. Because then my hold on you would be so much stronger, and you couldn't get away so easily. My darling I want you so much. I need you to guide me, to love me, to comfort me when I'm hurt, to be proud of me, to laugh with me to talk to me. I've got to have you, Pops. I've really got to. Please still love me.

Tuesday morning 9:50

Gee I wish I could see you. I wonder if I'll get to see you today. It's getting so bad missing you that everything anyone says reminds me of you. And I'm afraid to go to sleep because I dream of you, sometimes of having you, but it's lots worse when I dream of losing you. It's so hard to see you in my dreams and then wake up and not have you. Oh I miss you so much, and just seeing you 13 minutes is so hard. I love you pops, my darling Popsie. I love you so much.

I have just seen you. You damn two-timer. I always knew I couldn't trust you. Well, a lot of things have come out in this case, about father and now about you. What's the handkerchief for? Poor Pete. Oh darling, why do you have to do things like that? I love you so much I'm always afraid you're going to leave me, then you two time me. Oh Popsie I love you so much. But that dark card fortune-teller — she said, and everything she says happens — that you and I would be separated. Darling, it worries me. I couldn't bear to be really separated from you.

I've got to marry you. I'm so afraid that the things I'm making will never get into our house or our trailer. I'd like to seal the joint in Flintridge. Dear Otto says that the Washington Finance co. will probably be sold. Why did Pete and Tommy break up? I love you. Oh Popsie why did that fortune teller say we were going to be separated? I love you so much my darling Popsie. I just got your nice angry letter. Oh I adore you, I love you, I could never stop loving you and wanting to marry you.

I don't give one small damn about the relatives. My greatest pleasure will be in telling them "thanks folks, go to hell and meet my husband Mr. Gollum." Please Pops, you are more than just a man you are part of me and I could never wound that part of me by thinking of another man. Please darling, I love you. You're so masterful. I worship you. Pop the only time I'll brush you off is when you have lint on you. Don't brush me off. Please Pops, I love you so much. The reason I don't write about "certain" things is because I'm still inhibited I guess.

Pops, <u>I like everything you've ever done to me.</u> I like it all very much. The Hell with Yvonne. I told her that, mentally, that day at home, Monday was it, when she said I shouldn't have my picture taken with you and it "would be all right" for me to sleep with you provided I did it undercover. What is wrong with <u>the handkerchief?</u> Blood! Is it yours pops? And lipstick! So! Oh darling, please save your <u>love and blood for me.</u> What's wrong with your teeth? Do they hurt?

Oh pops, do you hurt somewhere? Is something wrong?

I do so want to have your children. I so want to see you as a "proud papa." Oh darling I want children like you so much that it hurts. I adore you, I worship you. Pops I promise that I will always be faithful and true to you and that I will always love you and appreciate you more and more. My darling. My pops. I adore you forever, but I still don't think you love me as much.

Your adoring, Louise.

————

A – 6 4-21-47 35 D.I.J.
34 D.T.T.
My darling Louise Baby, I love you.
In case I forget to ask you when I see you, was Mr. Jacobs being funny when he said you wouldn't want to marry me after the trial was over? Or was he serious? If he was funny, I guess it is O.K. If he was being serious then I'm agin him. I saw Dee Holder last night. He is one of the four attorneys I like best. IIe seems to be a human being. Not just a hunk of legality in male clothing. I saw Mr. K. today. I finished the outline of days. I have been going over each day since Thursday 13 March with him. Remembering, as much as possible, what we did and what I did. One day at a time. That is one day at one session of notes. I think that you will be given a chance to read those notes before too long. Try remembering our actions from Friday morning when I picked you up and took you to school, until the time we were picked up. So that you can make corrections or changes as needed. I s'pose that Mr. J. has you doing that stuff already. I can't have knitting needles or any stuff like that. All I do all

day is; sleep until Gene, the 11 till 7 guard, comes around with chow and yells some corny cracks in my general direction. Then I wake up and wave my hand at him to let him know I haven't done the Dutch. He leaves and I sleep, dreaming of you, until around 8, then I up and put on pants and jacket instead of a shirt – comb he hair, brush the pearls, pry open the eyes, make the bed and lie down. Read – think of you – write about 20 or 30 pages – both sides of notebook paper to you – 44 round trips of the tank to the mile – eat an orange – dream of you – throw my cup of dish water down the commode – dream of you – lie down – dream of Butch for 20 minutes – write about you. Write to you – talk to the guys – jerks that is; dream about you, - eat at 3:30 – nibble that is.

Then around 4:30 to 5:30 I expect your notes. Notes that is too. I wish they would become letters. Do you need paper? Wish I could give you some spare time. Gee honey, I miss you something terrible. Taint but 9 days "till April 30. Happy birthday my beloved darling. Happy, happy birthday, dearest. Maybe it's a bit previous but I want you to know that if we were free you would be my wife on the 30th of April at 12:01 in the morning. I sure wish we could be married in here. Guess that the attorneys won't let us be married in here. Wish they would tho – I wish to you, my God, that we could get married in here now. That is a bad wish I guess. Well at least you, I here, can't get away from me physically. And I am positive and sure that you will be with me in love for the rest of our lives. I love you my dearest. I adore you with all my power to tell you or to write. I wish I could get in contact with my mental telepathy. Then you could read in my mind the fact that I adore you and no one but you is ever in my thoughts. You are the only female in the world. There are no exceptions. All others are neuter gender.

Oh my dear I love you, I want you. I don't want you to go out on bail. Unless you want to. We are half way to the trial now, 35 days on Tuesday we have been in. 34 days til the trial. I would very much like for you to be out. At the same time, I like to see you, an understatement, and I like to get notes from you, another understatement. I love you. Still you have to make your own decision about going out on bail. I've been having fun telling all the boys here that you don't go out on bail because you don't want to be so far away from me. Regardless of that, you will still have to make the decision. I feel so futile trying to pour my heart out to you and not being able to use any but the same old stereotyped words, the same old phrases. It sounds as if I did not have much sense. I just wish I could tell what I really want to say – my life is yours – my life, my love, my body, my brain, my faith my soul - they are yours. I have no more to give. I have nothing more. Everything I am is yours. All that I will ever have is yours. Yours to do with as you will. If you want to pull out all the hair on my chest, and on junior – they are yours to pull. If you want to slug me, I am yours to slug – anything my dear. If you want me to love, to have and to cherish, that is what I want. I want your love as you have mine. I am pretty sure I have it. I pray that your relatives and others won't talk you away from my love. Your letters show that they are trying. Even in jail. Wonder if they don't realize, or don't' want to realize, that together we are strong – separated we are weakened. That isn't just prose either. I mean that – that is what my attorneys have told me – our cases are stronger together. Of course they, the attorneys, are for me a little stronger than for you. I keep telling them that you are the most important. Bus ask Mr. J if our cases are strongest together or apart – and if apart why? I sure am glad you plead <u>not guilty</u> and not a double plea of <u>not guilty and not guilty by reason of insanity.</u> If you had done the latter or if you ever do change your plea to the not guilty by reason of insanity, you can start looking for a prospective husband - I'll be in San Quentin. No kidding, that's the deal. But as it is now we both have the same chance and deal. Thank you very much honey – by the way that plea can only be change if you agree in open court.

In case you are wondering I am not worried. I know that whatever you do will be what you think is best. You are almost eighteen my dearest, I know you don't like a lecture but just the same, you are going to have a lot of additional authority, and responsibility after the 30th of April. Your ideas and your wishes will be those of a responsible person not just the voice of a minor. You have from then forward the power to control your life. To an almost complete degree. Most especially when we, or rather when <u>you</u> are released from here. Your ideas and wishes become your prerogative. My dearest you have already stated that your answer to my question " Will *you marry me?" was "Yes." I am going to ask you again. Now that you are of legal age or at least almost of legal age. Anyway; -* ˈ

My darling, I love you with all my heart and soul. I want you. I want you to marry me. I want you to be the mother of my children. I want you to be with me for the rest of our natural lives – and if there is an after life, I want you to be with me into eternity.

<u>*Will you marry me?*</u> *Please answer that question again.*

I will never let you go, my dear. If you said "yes" again to my question I will just warn you to remember what you are in for. If you said "no" or even hesitated a little bit, and are thinking of another man, or men, I must warn you that I will kill any other man that you ever take up with – as husband or even acquaintance. I am so sure of you that I am going to presume that you said "Yes." In fact Hooray – I'm going to get married!

Your faithful and ever loving Husband-to-be
George (Bud) Popsie (Mrs. Louise Overell
Gollum) Gollum.
4-22-47 – 8:30 P.M. I just re-wrote these first 3 pages and I think they are what I want to say pretty much.

———

B 1 4-21-47

My Louise darling;
    I have a cell alone now. The man who was with me is gone. What I did before in bed, I am now free to do as I want in the way I want. I get down on my knees each night and pray to <u>you.</u> That's right, I pray to you. <u>You are my God.</u>

I pray to you and I wonder and am humble before the vision of you. I wonder that you ever said "Yes" to me. I am humble that you love me, return my love and because of our love you have allowed me your body and I have given you mine. I am eternally and forever grateful to you for the wonders and delights that you have allowed me. You not only gave me your body, you gave me your brain and your soul. Because of our love for each other I have taken you, I have used your brain, I have tried to make you use my brain and I think I have. Before we gave ourselves to each other I believe you were a virgin. I swear to you that I was. Yes my dearest, never before in my life have I taken a woman. And I shall never take anyone else but you. This giving of ourselves one to the other, in the light of our love is good, my dearest. This shows to me that our love is a true and trustful, faithful and all-enduring love. I hope it shows the same to you.

When I pray to you each night I hope I will, and try to, reach into your mind and into your brain. In an attempt to make you realize by the very strength of my thought, the power of my feelings in my love for you.

If I could only direct the power and control the direction of my thought, I am sure that I could make you feel as I feel that our love is strong and good. That our love is powerful and all-enduring. That our love is more than average love. For I believe that our love is one which this world has never had before. A love simple and direct and at the same time complex and unlimited.

I have no fears that our love will win out to stand triumphant and reveal this fact before the ones who would destroy it. And there are those who would. There are those who would destroy what they don't understand. There are vandals who try to destroy beauty. This is to me, and to you I think, a wonderful thing of beauty. This is being written around 11:30 at night. I opened the cell door and wet over to the tank bars and turned the light on. There are two they just unscrew at night.

I just got your Sunday note. You say that "Everyone" tells you that you have lost me, who is everyone? Why do you believe, or even listen to them? In case you have wondered, I have been trying to get us married right here in jail. Ask Mr. Kaufman – He says "not good"

Would I marry if you were broke? I don't like that question. I am tired of people telling me I am after your money. And when you do it, it's too much. I'm going to ask you to tie your money up in some way so that I can't get hold of and you won't give me any - throw it away if you want.

*But for Christ's sake please stop telling me I'm a Gold Digger. I love you, not for your money. Think back on our plans. The trailer – the night of April 29th, our plans for it. When those plans were made did you have any money? Now, since the tragedy, the picture has changed. No by Gosh! This is going to be my last long letter maybe. I'll just send you short little love notes. I don't see what Mr. Jacobs is afraid of about that. After this one there will be no reference to our case or to any of those things suspicious to them Just little notes saying I love you. ** But I still can't see what is wrong with a love note. You do love me you say. The papers had it spread all over them too. So even if they start reading the notes, so what? If you ever leave me I'll sue for breach of promise. By the way, the matron thinks you don't appreciate her giving you the notes, or carrying yours. Please smile at here once in a while. I was told she asked you something about having an answer all ready when you got my note so she wouldn't have to make two trips or something. Ha ha! Do just as you please tho. Nuts to 'em. I'll help send their kids through college after we get out free.*

*I sure hope my last night's note did not upset you too much, or make you mad. If it made you mad you will probably draw back into that shell. I don't want that I pray that did not happen. Please don't shell over again. *** My baby darling, dearest one, I adore you, your lovely hair, your eyes, your nose, your lips, your ears, and your beautiful face, your wonderful neck. I like to see you naked my dear. I like to feel your warm body pressed close to my naked body. I like to hold your beautiful breasts in my hands and hold them tightly, cruelly. I like to suck hard on your wonderful nipples, and bite them a little. I like to run my hands down your body and between your legs. I like to bury my face in Butch. I am going to do that too. I like the taste of your beautiful, wonderful Butch fluids. I like your legs around me squeezing me tight. I like to run my tongue over your calves, up your legs over your beautiful buttocks, up your back in your ears. I like to breathe hotly into your ears and feel your hands on me, and Butch and Junior together.*

Oh my darling, my wonderful beautiful dearest baby, I love you. Please answer me, will we soon be together to do this? To share of each other's company? We will be, my dear. If not through the process of law then the *other way. I can, and will, manage to contain myself until the trial is over. But not any longer. Then I am going to claim you as my bride. And I pray you will still want to claim me as your husband. Please want me as your husband. From your letters I think you still have some inhibitions. Am I right? Is that why you won't tell me about your medical exam? Is that why you say " feel your leg etc.?" Why the etc? Remember me? I'm the guy whose going to marry you, and love your, and cherish you till <u>Death</u> do us part. And old man Death is about 50 years away for both of us. I <u>dare you</u> to stow your inhibitions away for a minute or two and tell me what you want do to me and have me do to you. Please my dearest one do that in your next and maybe your last letter.*

—————

Dearest Baby.

    Please don't forget for a minute that it is because I love you so much, because I am <u>not</u> to be away from you for any longer that absolutely necessary that the life insurance has been taken out. If we are declared <u>not</u> guilty there will be nothing done. It is only in the event that we are <u>not acquitted</u> that the Life Insurance will go into effect. Remember that. Don't tell Jacobs about the insurance, please.

Also remember, I will not leave here without you. regardless of how I go you are going too.

Don't forget, too, that after we are declared not guilty, and come back here for our property, don't let anyone spirit you away. <u>I</u> am going to drive you from here on, or you me, no one else. We aren't going to be separated again. Please see that they don't get you away without me. If they tell you I know where you are going, don't believe them unless I tell you I do.

You are mine and I have you now or forever more, my dearest. Don't leave me or let anyone take you away. PLEASE with all my heart, <u>(Junior too.)</u>
                                   Your husband-to-be (I said it, so there).

—————

4-22-47 34 *D.T.T.*

35D.I.J.
Halfway to trial By Gosh

My beloved Louise,

<u>*I love you.*</u>

*I have been ready for our visit since 7:00 this morning. I have show-
ered, the red socks on. The blue shorts. A clean "T" shirt, shaved. The
black shoes are shined. And Now I wait, and hope, soup just came in – It
must be around 10:15. Mr. K. told me yesterday that we would see each
other today. I hope he was not just joking. I love you, my dearest. I am
going to try to bruise your breasts or Butch or leave a mark in you some
way today. You say you are going to scratch me. I hope you do. Make it a
good deep one please! I hope I get a chance to bruise you. Just a mark on
one of our private places, your breast or Butch. A place where only you
will know about it. And where you can feel it. When you want.*

The guard just called - Here I come my dearest darling. My wife to be.

*What's the matter my dearest? I've just returned to the damned cell
from seeing you. Why wouldn't you let me put my hands on you?*
*My dearest have you been "reading the books" and not <u>me?</u> Why
won't you tell me what goes on?*

*Look – about Sunday Mar. 2. Don't 'you realize that this is a murder
case? Those attorneys of ours are trying to get us acquitted. They seem
to be doing a good job, but don't let them break us apart in the process.
Remember back to what Mr. J. said "the girl was Beulah." (That's <u>you</u>
my dear.) Remember this. In a case like this, it is often necessary for odd
things to happen – or to be found out. Some truth – some fiction. I am
going to tell you something. It is the truth. As and if you love me, and you
do I believe, I have always been truthful to you and now is no exception.
Since I have been going with you, I have never been unfaithful to you. I
have never been unfaithful in any way, word, thought, or deed. On my*

honor I swear this. I swear it on my love for you which is confined only by my own body size.

I can say nothing more than this. I am sorry, and a pretty good bit hurt by the fact, that you think I was with another girl on March 2nd. I swear to you I was not. Maybe I was not there either, (yet).

You should see Junior right now. He's thinking about Butch, and other parts of you, and he's so proud of himself he's all swollen up.

Hey, Baby, about this relation business. I don't give a damn if <u>you</u> think your relatives are the best in the world and mine are the worst, or vice-versa. Or what <u>I</u> think about both sets of relatives – and I am marrying <u>you</u>, and you are marrying <u>me</u>. I ain't marrying your damn relatives – and you aren't marrying my damn relatives – any of them. So, nuts to them all. As soon as we are married and together, as far as I'm concerned, we won't have any relatives form either side. Just acquaintances, no more, no less, period.

I want you right now my dear. I want us to be together, free, and married <u>right this instant.</u> I do so much wish that we were. We would be by now, if that damn Chief of Police Hodgkinson and Sheriff Mussick hadn't gotten bright ideas. <u>Damn them to hell!</u> I love you, we sure will be acquitted, I hope. If we aren't, then <u>our</u> Life Insurance goes into effect. Now I imagine you know what Life Insurance is, N'est-ce pas??

My most dear baby doll, all I've been thinking about is how happy I'm going to be when we are together again, only married this time. The general concensus of opinion down here is 'That only whores and movie actresses dye their hair." You aren't any or either of these types. Why on earth do you want to dye that which is so doggone nice, and wonderful, and beautiful now? And perhaps be classified b others, as one of those people? You know my darling that if you really want to dye it, it would be alright. With me. I guess I would get used to it. But even so, and if your mind is really made up that you want to and must, even if I don't like it, please wait'till we are outside and get a professional job. I still wish you *wouldn't . I always have to hurry the last few pages, or word, on one of the communications. I never seem to have enough time to finish them leisurely. I write all day on and off and still never seem to get said what I want. Some of the days when we are together after the trial, I'll tell you all about what I have wanted to say in these notes, and never been able to put into writing. I'll do it some day though it'll be verbal.. I'll spend the rest of my life trying to make you the happiest mortal on the face of the earth. I will succeed too. <u>I WILL SUCCEED</u>. Even if I do yell at you once in a while.*

With all my love
Your husband,
Popsie

———

During their last few days of freedom before their arrest, Bud and Louise had exhibited behavior totally inconsistent with what would be normal. Family members were astonished by their lack of grief; particularly on the part of Louise. While they were also, to an extent, surprised by the arrest, it explained their behavior. It made it very difficult for the two families to rally around the young couple. It was a particularly difficult situation for the Jungquists. Their daughter, sister and aunt had been murdered and Louise, their granddaughter, cousin and niece was accused of the murder. The Jungquists were, and probably still are, a stalwart family with strong family bonds. They **did** rally around Louise and, inasmuch as they were tried together, around Bud. The Rectors, particularly Wilafred and Wilhelmina Stomel, nee Rector, also got in the accused couples corner. George and Minnie Rector were advanced in age and probably weren't as involved as the others. The Overells had been close friends, and they were grief stricken as were the Jungquists. The fact is that the evidence was strong and both families had to have had lingering doubts.

Bud and Louise would sit in jail for three months and five days before their trial began. This was good for the prosecution. They used the time in gathering evidence and strengthening their case; and it was a strong case. But that also gave the defense time to come up with the means to create doubt in the jurors' minds. As is sometimes the case, the murders were so brutal and cold blooded that it could be difficult for some people to believe that a daughter could be induced to participate. The jury would come from Orange County, a conservative law abiding citizenry. Most of the pool would come from families where there is love and with strong religious beliefs. It would be inconceivable for some to accept what the State was claiming. It was something they could more easily accept if it had occurred in a less afflu-ent family. This is not a rational belief but a pervasive one…even today.

Much of the time was spent in various motions that would affect the trial; the most important one was the defense's effort to separate the trial. The prosecution resisted vigorously. Gollum's attorneys were also aboard on the attempt to sever the trials even though he would prove to be the least sympathetic defendant in the eyes of the public and probably the jury. With separate trials it would be difficult for the prosecution to fix the blame for the actual act of killing. The state was trying them for conspiracy and would not have the burden of proving who actually swung the hammer and set off the explosion.

Another thing that delayed the start of the trial was due to Chief Hodg-kinson's request for the Attorney General to appoint a prosecutor.

During this wait, Bud and Louise were visited regularly by their fami-lies. Even though the two families had been close for many years there was a natural desire for their family member to be less guilty than the other family member involved in the trial. This was kept simmering beneath the surface until the trial actually began. In reading the pretrial letters, it is apparent that there was a schism, small at first, growing between Bud and Louise and this was probably effected at the same time it reflected the schism between the two families.

On April 28th, Judge Franklin denied the defense motion to separate the trial and set the trial to begin on May 26th. The long wait for the trial would soon end. Even without the trial, the papers were assiduously covering it on a daily basis.

Even before the letters were made public, the decades long friendship between the Overells, Jungquists and Rectors was crumbling. Louise's uncles, Emmanuel and Fred, and their families, were putting pressure on Louise to distance herself from Bud – both legally and emotionally. The same was hap-pening to a degree with the attorneys. Jacobs was sure he could get Louise off if not encumbered with Gollum. Kaufman probably was sure of that too and preferred them to be tried together. Had the prosecution known that they were going to have such a tough time, they most likely would have severed the trial and made a deal with Louise. At some point, there is no doubt that Louise had moved totally away from Bud emotionally, but to make any kind of deal, she would have to admit the murders and her involvement even if it was a result of pressure from Bud. She never was able to do that. It's possible, (it sometimes happens with mentally disturbed offenders) that she had convinced herself that she did not do it.

The Rectors and Stomels had no choice but to accept the defense position that the two were innocent. They knew that any guilt would lie most heavily on Bud. Interaction between Bud's mother and grandparents, and the Jungquists ceased. Mr. and Mrs. Overell provided the nexus for the relationship anyway and with them gone there was nothing much left.

The public exposure of the letters was a shock to both families. While they certainly weren't surprised that the couple had been intimate, it was unspoken and unacknowledged (This was 1947, a different time in America.), the lewdness and crass language was a shock to them. The Jungquists saw this as evidence of Bud's unwholesome influence over Louise. They were right.

The letters/notes tell a lot about the two defendants; particularly about Bud since he wrote the most letters, and his letters were verbose and repetitive; and some were disgustingly graphic. It is impossible to tell exactly when the split became complete. The seeds were planted, certainly, but it would appear that it actually happened during the trial since they seemed to be a unit when the trial began. What was clear was that there was pressure from Louise's family for her to pull away from him emotionally and, from her attorneys, to split from him in the trial. All the information and messaging between the two was obviously not limited to the written dialogue. The two families were certainly trying to influence them.

Bud's letters show a mild tendency for sadistic sex[6], a domineering personality as illustrated by his frustration over his inability to prevent Louise from dyeing her hair. He was a pseudo-intellectual and a would-be manipulator; a combination of an insecure egomaniac[7].

---

6 http://www.psychologistanywhereanytime.com/sexual_problems_pyschologist/
psychologist_sadomasochism.htm

7 http://www.relationship-affairs.com/what-is-an-egomaniac-and-egocentric-behaviour.
html

> *While they appear to be super-confident, any criticism destroys the ego-maniacs. They'd rather be doing the criticism. Because they over-empha-sise [sic] every little achievement on their part, they also tend to take lack of achievement/criticism very, very badly.*

His spelling and sentence structured suggests that far from a genius, he was not really average. His attempt at an intellectual description of their love and meta-physical meanderings are comical. Throughout the entire exchange, his anger, frustration and fear is manifest. He was losing control over a person whom he had persuaded to help kill her parents and now couldn't stop from dyeing and cutting her hair. His biggest fear was the growing likelihood of losing the fortune for which he had just brutally murdered two people.

His compulsive pornographic meanderings demonstrate an over active, if not perverted libido. It is difficult to determine if his redundant declara-tions of his love for Louise was real or just part of his attempt to convince her that he was not after her money. No one can read his mind but his descrip-tion of her beauty can only reflect an impression based on intense love or the crassest kind of insincerity. Louise, as he knew her before her pre-trial makeover is pictured here.

One of Bud's letters, not only points to his guilt but his stupidity. When he found that someone had obtained his pictures, he told Louise to ask Otto Jacobs, Louise's attorney, to remove some items from his car that the pros-ecution could use in their case. His amateurish efforts of being a con man are displayed in his pathetic effort to convince Louise that he did not need her money because an ex-shipmate was going to give him one third of his profit from the sale of his oil laden land in Oklahoma. The figure he used was $10 Million and the reason his friend was being so generous was because Bud had loaned him $600 while in the Navy. Both elements of the concocted story are not even remotely credible.

Louise was pathetic. It would appear that she was completely enthralled by his flattery. All her eighteen years she was made to feel that she was physically unattractive and now this handsome friend of the family introduced her to sex and told her she was beautiful. That, along with her resentment for passive abuse from her parents, induced her to take part in a heinous crime against her parents. It is evident, from the exchanges, that her family and attorney were pulling her out of Bud's web, as it were. The extrication had started at the beginning of the trial and obviously became complete by the end. Her slave-like adoration had become total aversion. She finally faced the reality of what she had done.

She resumed normalcy and that led to alcoholism and eventual destruction. Bud, on the other hand, had no problems with guilt and his long wasted life continued.

On Sunday, May 4th, the Jungquists held a meeting at the Manhattan Place home of Louise Jungquist, the matriarch of the family. The Jungquists; Fred, Emmanuel, his wife Eva, and the two daughters were all there. Fred Davey, husband of Yvonne Jungquist, (Fred's Jungquist's daughter) was also there. The meeting was to discuss how to handle the publication of the letters written in the jail between Louise and Bud. By now the lurid letters were on front pages all over the United States. The newspaper reading public was either shocked or titillated depending on the level of their tolerance or enjoyment of what was considered by some as pornography. The Jungquists, as were the Rectors, who were not invited to the meeting, were religious and refined people. They were more than shocked. They were ashamed and embarrassed. Neither Bud nor Louise was raised up to be involved in this kind of behavior.

After the perfunctory hugs, handshakes and small talk was over and all were seated in the spacious parlor, there were a few seconds of nervous silence. Everyone knew why they were there but no one wanted to be the first to bring it up. Emmanuel, the oldest, started it off.

"Well, it looks like Louise has put a nail in her coffin," Emmanuel said and immediately regretted his choice of words. "I'm sorry; I mean it's going to be difficult for Otto to find a sympathetic jury after this." Everyone shook their head in negative agreement. It was the unofficial feeling of the family that Bud had killed their sister, and daughter; (Louise Jungquist was in the room in her wheel chair, alert but not participating. Although it had been over a month she was still deeply feeling the grief over the death of her daughter.) When there were just two members of the family, occasionally, the possibility of them being guilty was mentioned, but in formal meetings, so to speak, as this one was, the family's position was that Bud had done it and Louise was only peripherally involved and protecting Bud. The influence he had over her was obvious to all that knew them.

"That's not Louise talking," Marjorie, Emmanuel and Ida's daughter, the cousin closest to Louise, declared in a semi angry tone, "that's Bud talking through her. I have known her all her life and I have never heard her utter a nasty word."

This brought about a chatter of agreement among the family members and comments about Bud Gollum.

Emmanuel interrupted the hubbub by slightly elevating is voice and saying, "It's done; the horse is out of the barn. We can't change the past. What we need to decide is what we do as a family. How do we handle this?"

There was a brief interlude of thoughtful silence. Next to the murders, if they were murdered, this was the worst thing that had ever happened in the family. Fred spoke next. "There isn't much we can do. We can't issue a public statement saying the Bud made her do it, or that she is different from the rest of us. Bud is a cancer in this family and when you have a cancer, you cut it out. Louise has to cut Bud out of her life. Apparently we can't separate the trials but we can certainly insist that Otto separate the defense."

This was obvious to the family and everyone voiced agreement. "Ok, now we start working on Louise. Gently at first but we must be ready to be forceful if she doesn't come around"

"What do you mean by forceful, Uncle Manny?" Yvonne asked.

"It's either us or Bud in the end; she will have to make that choice!"

Everyone agreed by nods and changing the subject to what few pleasant things was happening in the family at the time.

The Rectors had a similar meeting. Inside, they had drawn nearly the same conclusions regarding involvement as the Jungquists but they saw disaster for Bud if the couple was separated at this point; they needed to work in the opposite direction of the Jungquists.

After disclosure of the letters, communication between the two families ceased and their energy for the accused couple went through and was filtered and modified by the attorneys in a legal context.

Until the trials end, the couple while in court, was joined at the hip…at least for now.

Part II

THE TRIAL

O n June 24, 1947, the most notorious criminal trial in Orange County history began.

Seated at the desk at the right, are the trial attorneys, W.B Beirne, Z.B West, Jr., S.B. Kaufman, and Otto Jacobs. West and Jacobs represented Overell; Beirne and Kaufman represented Gollum.

It was to be a war between the attorneys from the jury selection through the trial; nearly every piece of evidence the prosecution presented was challenged. The jury selection took four weeks. over 500 jurists were called. Only one of the first 12 called was selected and she was later pulled because some-

one threatened her life if she voted for conviction.

The violence of the murder itself in such a setting; aboard a yacht in beautiful serene Newport Harbor attracted attention from the beginning. Newport Beach, through the years was, and has remained even with moderate growth, a low crime area. Their homicide rate averages less than 2 per year…and the Bay is out of the highest crime area. This may well have been the first homicide in the Bay and may, today, remain the only one.

The local media, including the Los Angeles papers was all over it. It was a natural; a young couple in love murdering her parents, who objected to marriage between the two, for early access to the family fortune. The leaking of the love letters, or notes, by the Los Angeles Examiner created a trial version of a "perfect storm." The Orange County Courthouse, now a museum, was swamped! Santa Ana is the county seat and the court house is pictured here.

The 1950 census set the population of Santa Ana at 48,651 souls. Orange County had started to be caught up in the post war growth by then so the population in 1947 was close to only 45,000. Most certainly, the downtown community and the Sheriff's Department, then called the Sheriff's Office, under the direction of Jim Musick, could not have been prepared for a 19 week trial with overflow crowds every day. As a 17 year-old high school boy the author got off the school bus every day in downtown Fontana, 50 miles away, borrowed a paper off the rack of the corner drug store and read the entire pre-trial proceedings of the day. The trial, itself was even more captivating. It was every bit as spectacular as the OJ trials, some 50 years later. It's difficult to understand how civilized people can see pleasure in watching a trial for a brutal double murder with two young people on trial for their lives. The little courthouse and court officers were hard pressed to handle the daily crowds.

Beulah Louise Overell and George Gollum engaged in an illicit, perverted, sadistic passion amounting almost to a frenzy…To gratify their passion, this couple killed her father and mother.

With these words, as printed in a local newspaper, the prosecutor in Santa Ana, Calif. opened the state's case against eighteen year-old Beulah Louise Overell and twenty one year-old George "Bud" Gollum. Californians reacted immediately to this lurid prose. Here was an almost official promise of a lot more than an ordinary homicide case. The little courthouse was soon mobbed. Sightseers came in droves, armed with fans and cushions and beady-eyed with anticipation. For twenty three weeks they sat agape in the gallery or queued up in impatient shifts. Some, unable to elbow their way in, tried brazen strategy on the guards or merely dawdled away the time on the lawn outside.[8]

PROSECUTION OPENING STATEMENT.

Ladies and gentlemen of the jury, it becomes my privilege and my function at this time briefly and without detail to outline to you the case which the prosecution intends to present for your consideration. Everything I state will be a matter which I expect we shall prove. As his honor will tell you, nothing which I will say constitutes evidence and is not to be regarded by you as evidence. It is simply that I am going to try to outline the prosecution's case for your assistance so that as the evidence comes in a little here and a little there it will place itself in your minds in relationship to the case as a whole and to the evidence as a whole. We expect to prove that Walter E. Overell, who was, I think, about 62 years of age and Beulah A. Overell, his wife, at the age of about 57 and their only child and daughter, Beulah Louise Overell, the defendant here, lived in a palatial home atop a hilltop in Flintridge near Pasadena, California.

Mr. and Mrs. Overell are now dead. We shall establish that they were murdered. No person other than the murderers so far as we know saw the crime committed. No witness will take the stand and say to you, "I saw it done." Nevertheless, strong, clear, and convincing proof will be made to enable you to answer the simple questions which a seeker for truth always asks when confronted by the tragedy of sudden and violent death. The questions what, how, where, when, why and who. What? Murder, premeditated, intended murder; not suicide, not accident, but murder. How? By multiple, repeated violent blows on the heads of the victims crushing and penetrating their skulls. In the case of Mrs. Overell we shall establish that the blows were struck by a ballpeen hammer or other blunt instrument of similar character and proportions. In the case of Mr. Overell we shall establish that he was killed by means of blows administered by a stanchion or pipe which we shall produce for your inspection. Where?

---

8 Life Magazine, September 1, 1947

They were murdered aboard the yacht Mary E as it lay in anchor at its mooring in Newport Harbor in Orange County, California. When? On Saturday, March 15, 1947.

Mrs. Overell was killed between 9:00 and 10:00 p.m. Mr. Overell was killed between 10:00 and 11:00 p.m. This we expect to establish.

Why? Why were they murdered? Because they were obstacles to the lust and greed of the murderers. Who? They were murdered by these defendants, the only child and heir, Beulah Louise Overell and her lover, George Rector Gollum.

Now I propose to recount briefly some of the evidence, some of the highlights of the evidence which will be presented to you. We shall show that on March 15 at about 7:00 to 7:15 a.m. the defendant Gollum was seen standing, apparently with nothing to do, at the Standard Oil dock which lies close to the mooring of the Mary E. When approached he left the scene. Later, sometime after 8:00 o'clock the Overells, Mr. and Mrs. Overell and their daughter, arrived and went on board the Mary E. During that day mechanics were brought on board and the Mary E was taken to a repair shop where some repair work was done. The day was spent in repairing the engine, the principal engine of the Mary E, grinding the valves, putting on a new fuel pump, and things of that sort. And during that day the parties involved, Mr. and Mrs. Overell and the defendants were on and off the boat at certain times. Mr. Overell and one of the mechanics took a trip to Santa Ana in an effort to acquire certain parts for the boat. The work continued until about 7:30 p.m. when, with the aid of the mechanics the boat was taken back to its mooring and at about 9:00 o'clock, the boat having been moored, the mechanics were taken to the shore by Mr. Overell, who took them in the little dinghy, the little rowboat which customarily rests on the top of the deck or the roof of the after-cabin and Mr. Overell left them at their place of business at about 9:30, exactly 9:30 I think we should put it, that evening.

During the time that Mr. Overell and the mechanics were gone the only persons left on that boat were the defendants and Mrs. Overell. Mr. Over-

ell got back about 10:00 o'clock, a few moments one way or the other. He and the defendants swung the dinghy on the davits up into its cradle on top of the after cabin.

We believe that you will reach the conclusion that at that time while that was being done by Mr. Overell who was up on deck with these two defendants, that Mrs. Overell's dead body lay on the floor of the forward-cabin. Mr. Overell started down the companionway into that cabin and at that moment was struck violently with the sharp end of this pipe or stanchions handled in this way, in a certain way to penetrate and puncture his skull on the left-hand side. Down into the companionway he fell down onto the floor below in the forward cabin and there was again repeatedly struck with the same instrument. They both lay there dead.

Dynamite had been acquired, we will produce evidence about that; electrical detonator caps had been acquired, we will produce evidence about that; a time clock had been prepared, and we will produce evidence about that. An effort was made to cover up the fact that murder had been committed on that boat by causing the boat to be exploded and sunk and so the dynamite was placed attached to the detonator cap and attached to a battery and attached to the time clock, set so that at 11:45 the contact would be made to the operation of the clock and the explosion would take place. This having been done, these defendants left the boat and went ashore.

Mr. Overell had brought out the dinghy and another boat to be used in getting to and from the shore. They used that boat and they went ashore. They say that they ate hamburgers. According to their statements, which we will produce, Mr. Gollum's appetite was not so good, but the defendant Beulah Louise Overell ate her hamburger and part of his.

On schedule the explosion took place. The boat blew up. It was partly wrecked. Two simultaneous blasts made holes, one on the portside of the boat in the after part of the forward cabin and another on the starboard side of the boat in the engine room and through those holes water came in and filled the entire forward cabin of the boat and it was partly sunk.

The Coast Guard arrived and others. The boat was beached in its partly sunk condition and an examination was made. The hatchway above the forward cabin was opened and shortly there appeared a foot, the foot of Mr. Overell floating in the water which was right up below the roof of the cabin. Mr. Overell's body was brought out and then in a short time there appeared some hair and somebody caught a hold of the hair ad it was the hair and the head of Mrs. Overell, and her body was brought out.

Later the boat was lifted onto the ways and the water was drained from it and experts went down to examine and find out the cause of the explosion and they found dynamite. A great deal of dynamite had not exploded, it had not been properly wired to the detonator so unexploded sticks of dynamite were there. Exploded pieces of detonator were there. Detonator wire was there. All of the indicia of a planned explosion, and explosion which was not accidental, which was planned, devised, and intended to destroy evidence of murder. That it was not successful was due both to ignorance and ineptitude of the murderer who used dynamite and did not wire it up properly so that it would all explode and did not know that dynamite doesn't set things on fire but puts fire out and consequently there was no fire to destroy the evidence of the murders.

Examination of the bodies established that both the victims died of wounds inflicted before and measurably before the time of the explosion of the dynamite. Incontrovertible evidence will be produced to establish that fact that both victims were dead before the dynamite was exploded and also that they were dead before the water rushed in and they were immerged in water.

Who planned and prepared and caused this explosion? The evidence will show that the defendants Gollum and Beulah Louise Overell together went to places where Gollum purchased dynamite and detonator caps, not the one place but two places, not one trip but more than one trip in which they accompanied one another and the purchases were made.

It will be proved that Gollum prepared the alarm clock which was used as the device to set off the explosion. It will be proved that Gollum experimented with explosions of dynamite.

It will be proved that Gollum and Beulah Louise Overell and Mr. and Mrs. Overell were the only persons known to have been on or near the boat at the times involved in the murders.

After the explosion the defendants hovered about until they made sure that both victims were definitely dead and then without waiting to see her parents they left. They did not go to her grandmother's home where she had a room, where she would be chaperoned. They went up to the vacant Overell mansion on top of the hill in Flintridge and there spent the night alone and within the next day or two we will show you these defendants rummaging the house, opening and searching the safe looking for papers, planning their wedding and talking business until they were arrested a few days later. That and other conduct which will be produced in detail to you will appear so cold-blooded, so unnatural as to bear on its very face the earmarks of guilt, what we lawyers call consciousness of guilt and will show on the part of these defendants an abandoned and malignant heart and in addition to that we shall show in detail and beyond controversy the existence of the most powerful motive for murder known to human heart.

We shall prove that these defendants were engaged and had been engaged in an illicit, perverted, sadistic, sexual passion amounting to a frenzy; that her parents definitely and unequivocally objected to their marriage, definitely and unequivocally threatened that if she undertook to marry against their consent that she would be disinherited and so was added to this frenzied passion the element of greed. This we will establish beyond controversy.

These individuals, Mr. and Mrs. Overell, constituted an obstacle to the fulfillment of the desires of these defendants and they were removed. We had lust, we had greed, we had frustration.

Ladies and gentlemen, these are the raw materials out of which murders are made. In short, we shall prove the corpus delicti, the body of the crime, the elements, the necessary elements to the crime of murder, namely, dead bodies, death produced by criminal agency, and we shall establish that these defendants were the criminal agency, in concert, together, working equally. We shall prove that it was murder, not accident, not suicide, murder; that the defendants planned, prepared and committed the murders and the subsequent explosion the purpose of which was only to cover up the fact of crime.

This evidence will be by means of witnesses, laymen, just ordinary people who saw something, heard something; police officers, doctors, experts of one kind or another; people who have examined the boat, examined the dynamite, examined the wires, examined bloodstained clothing, examined the instruments of death and who will come in and report their findings.

We shall produce photographs showing many salient features of this case. We shall produce for your consideration articles of physical evidence, the death weapons, the wires, and many of the articles of physical evidence. Bits of evidence here, there, and the other place, which fit together into a common picture. We shall produce letters and statements of the defendants, admission on their part, not confession but admission to certain things and by these measures, this type of evidence, we shall prove as against these defendants, and each of them opportunity, planning and preparation, motive and unnatural acts and conduct showing consciousness of guilt.

We shall put you full in possession of the answers to the questions what, how, where, when, why, who and we shall also put you in possession of the answer to the one further question, which is dominant in this case, who stood to gain by these murders.

That will be the prosecution's case.

The attorneys for both defendants declined to make an opening state-ment but reserved the right to do so at a later time. They did not make an opening statement because they weren't sure at this point what their plan would be; it was in the developmental stage. Jacobs was disappointed by not being able to separate the trials. He was sure he could get Louise off, if tried alone, by focusing on the more probable guilt of Bud. They began by chal-lenging every bit of evidence or testimony the prosecution presented.

STATE KEY WITNESSES.

Captain Thomas McGaff, commander of the Orange County Sheriff Depart-ment Bureau of Records and Identification supervised the crime scene inves-tigation and received all the physical evidence which he turned over to Ray H. Pinker Criminalist for the Los Angeles Police Department. The OCSD, in 1947, did not have a crime lab - this was true of most sheriff departments of that size. Chain of possession in evidence is critical in trials because of the possibility of tampering. Captain McGaff, an honest and capable officer, was not the most competent witness. One of the problems in effective law enforcement is that low crime means the lack of expertise in managing it when it happens. Captain McGaff probably did not have a lot of experience in testifying in high profile murder cases. McGaff was the state's number one witness and the defense attacked him like barracudas. They forced him to admit that 14 different investigators had access to Gollum's car from which the most critical evidence was taken. The chain of possession of the evidence was challenged for every item of evidence. It is vital in criminal cases that evidence be maintained as found at the scene. Precise records of every per-son who handled the evidence must be kept to prevent tampering. It is pos-sible that the Sheriff's Department may have been sloppy in preserving the chain of possession of some of the evidence.

Ray Pinker from LAPD analyzed all the physical evidence. His most important testimony was that a blood spot on a board taken from the boats engine room had to have been dried before the boat was flooded. This was a key factor. This proved that the injury producing the blood took place at least 20 minutes before the explosion. He also testified that the blood on Bud and Louise's clothing was the same blood type as Mrs. Overell. Pinker had a great deal of trial experience and could not be shaken. The defense claimed the blood grouping was uncertain and may not have been the same type as

Walter Overell. It's sad that DNA analysis was not around at that time. DNA would have undoubtedly convicted the couple.

Dr. John J. Montanus, conducted the second autopsy and testified that the cause of death of both victims was blunt force trauma that crushed their skulls and both were dead at the time the boat was flooded because of the explosion.

Dr. John D. Decker agreed with the three previous medical experts that Mr. and Mrs. Overell were dead before the explosion and that they died from blows to the head by a piece of pipe or a stanchion. He testified that he drew his conclusions from his experience with the effects of high explosives on the human body as a combat surgeon with the army.

An official from the Trojan Powder Company testified that the dynamite and caps found on the Mary E after the murders were purchased from them.

A hand writing expert who testified that the handwriting on the Trojan Powder Company-issued receipt for the explosives was that of George Gollum.

Mary Pritchett, the maid, testified that she saw Bud opening up locked storage compartments with keys that Mrs. Overell always kept on her person, never giving them to anyone. Bud would have had to take them from her body. The keys were found on Bud's key ring when he was arrested. She also testified that Bud and Louise were in a celebratory or jovial mood the following morning.

A neighbor, Mrs. Herbert Van Zwoll testified as to Bud and Louise's cavalier attitude immediately after the murders.

Louise's Uncle Emmanuel Jungquist, brother of the victim, Beulah Jungquist Overell, testified that he read an entry in Louise's diary saying "I get so mad at mother, I could kill her." He also testified that she told him two days after the murders that she wanted Bud to be president of the Washington Finance Company, one of Overell's holdings.

Fred Davey, husband of Louise's cousin, Yvonne, daughter of Fred Jungquist, testified of the accused couple's inappropriate behavior – that is behavior inconsistent with grief.

Two of Bud's class mates from Los Angeles City College testified for the prosecution. Philip Edward Mason testified that when he asked Gollum what his attraction was for Louise he mentioned her parents being listed in the above described "Southwest Bluebook." Lester James Nelson, Jr., a shipmate and longtime friend testified that Bud told him that the Overells objected to the marriage and threatened to cut Louise out of her inheritance.

The defense called a few witnesses such as military explosion experts who would testify as to how explosion would move bodies around but they were insignificant. In the face of overwhelming circumstantial evidence and a good amount of physical evidence, the defense, guided by Louise's principal attorney, Otto Jacobs, decided not to challenge the fact that Gollum purchased the dynamite but claim that he purchased it at the request of Walter Overell; his purpose being to commit suicide because of failing business or to blow up the Mary E because he was convinced he had made a poor selection and wanted to recoup his loss via insurance. The theory would be that it blew up accidentally while he was setting it up. It was an uphill battle all the way. Such behavior was inconsistent with Walter Overell's character and, in fact, he was still in good shape financially. They had no way of proving that and, in fact, they did not try. The prosecution had no way of disproving it. The theory was put out there solely for the purpose of giving the jury something upon which to base their "reasonable doubt"

Kaufman, Gollum's lead attorney was very capable but there was no doubt about who was in charge. It was Otto A. Jacobs, Louise's lead attorney. The other two, Beirne and West, both excellent attorneys, were there primarily to make sure nothing was missed. They could be compared to the so called "Dream Team of O. J. Simpson fame; every bit as competent and just as unethical. To make his scenario even possible, he had to first discredit the state's case. He had to disprove the strong case that the Overells would not approve of the marriage and would cut Louise out of their will and he had to disprove that Bud crushed Walter and Beulah's heads and set off the dynamite. Actually, he did not have to prove anything. He just had to create reasonable doubt. Unfortunately, "reasonable" is not quantifiable and what he did was create "unreasonable" doubt in a style and to a degree that would set the bar for later trials such as the O.J. Simpson, Robert Blake, Michael Jackson and Casey Anthony trials. None of these trials surpassed it.

Every piece of evidence the state presented was challenged. Even after they decided to have Gollum admit that he purchased the dynamite, they spent hours trying to discredit the handwriting expert who identified it as Gollum's. They admitted it was Gollum's signature and then challenged the expert opinion of the witness who agreed with them! The purpose, of course was to discredit the prosecutors. The prosecuting attorneys were put on trial!

OVERELL TESTIMONY.

Louise Overell was on the stand for two days. The sole purpose of her testimony was to state for the jury that she did not kill her parents and to say that her parents did not oppose her marriage to Bud Gollum. They had her make a drawing of the floor plan of the home in Flintridge with circles and arrows for no purpose other than to tire out the jury and perhaps to make Louise appear as a sympathetic figure – a young woman shamefully accused by the state of the horrendous and unlikely crime of beating her parents to death with a hammer and pipe. It's interesting that Otto Jacobs never asked Louise any questions, not one, about her involvement in the purchase of the dynamite. Bud was left hanging out alone on that issue. Jacobs was preparing for a motion to declare none of the evidence against Gollum to be relevant to the case against Overell. Bud had to realize that he was out of the picture as far as the inheritance was concerned but was fighting for survival.

The defense continued their barrage of redundancy with Gollum on the stand but his examination was much more germane to the trial than that of Miss Overell. His testimony was nearly 100 pages long. One of the purposes of his testimony was to paint a picture of a typical American boy who had served his country. Kaufman did a good job. He also brought out an interesting account of the activities of Saturday, March 15, 1947, the day of the murders. He covered everything from the day before when Gollum purchased the explosives, his arrival at Balboa the next day, the activity of everyone throughout the day up to and including the explosion, and Gollum and Miss Overell's activity until the day of their arrest. Gollum did a good job as a witness. He obviously had no problem with lying. Mr. Williams' cross examination was weak.

GOLLUM TESTIMONY.

The following is taken from the transcripts of his testimony regarding the purchase of the explosives:

....Testimony covering Gollum's picking up Overell at school and fixing her lunch at his home....

Q And where were you in the house?

A In the kitchen.

Q And during that time you were in the kitchen, did anything occur?

A Yes, the telephone rang.

Q And who answered it?

A I did.

Q And Louise was still in the kitchen?

A She was.

Q And where was the telephone in their home with reference to the kitchen?

A Through the dining room and down a short hall.

Q It was in the hall in the forepart of the house, was it?

A In the after part of the house.

Q And what happened when you answered the phone?

A A person said "This is Mr. Overell" and asked for me.

Q And what did you say?

A I identified myself and Mr. Overell—

Q Did you recognize the voice?

A It sounded like his voice, yes.

Q *And what was said? Just tell about the conversation that you had at that time.*

A *Well, he asked about my family and I told him that everyone was alright, and I asked about how Mrs. Overell was, and he said "fine," and I asked him how he was and he said "fine," and then he asked if I would do a favor for him and I said "certainly," and he asked if I would purchase approximately 50 pounds, or he said "about 50 pounds of dynamite for him," and I said I did not know if I could or not, I had never had anything to do with dynamite, but I asked him if you did not have to have a license to buy dynamite, and he said that he did not know but he did not think so and I told him I would call around and find out if I could purchase it and call him back and he said that he was having luncheon at the club and did not know when he was going to return to the office so if I was able to get it I should bring it up that evening when I brought "Bill," which was a nickname he had for Louise,.....*

Q *Was there anything said in that conversation about caps?*

A *Yes, he mentioned that he would like some electric caps and he asked me to tell no one that he was purchasing dynamite for him.*

Q *That is the substance of the conversation?*

A *That is.*

Q *Now, subsequently to that conversation, did you return to the kitchen?*

A *I did.*

Q *And did you tell Miss Overell about the call?*

A *Yes.*

Q *And what did you do thereafter?*

A Well, I got the classified and looked under, I believe under explosives, and I called several numbers and finally called, I believe it was the Trojan Powder Company in the directory, and the individual, I don't remember whether it was a lady or a man said that it cost $18.75, I believe it was, a hundred weight, and that they had a magazine at Chatsworth and that the electric caps were available there at the magazine.

Q And after that did you have a question with your mother or stepfather about you going to Chatsworth?

A I did and I asked them where Chatsworth was and they told me they had a map and told me where to find it and I got it and looked up Chatsworth in it.

Q And thereafter what did you and Louise do?

A Well, I asked Louse to go with me and we went out to Chatsworth.

Q And what time did you leave the house?

A I think it was about 2:30.

Q Do you recall about what time you arrived at Chatsworth?

A About 3:30.

Q Tell us what happened at Chatsworth.

A I parked the car in the yard. I first had to ask the way to the magazine, and then after I finally got there I parked the car in the yard of Mr. Hill's house and went inside - - He came out and he and I went back inside, and I told him that I was after some dynamite, and he asked me what percentage I wanted and I said I did not know, that it was not for me, I was getting it for someone else and I did not know what the person wanted it for so he suggested a 40% dynamite as a general all around percentage, and he asked if I wanted any fuses and I told him that I had been asked to get electric caps and he said that they were fuses and they came in various lengths and he asked me if I knew what lengths I wanted and I said no so he suggested 4 foot lengths. He then asked me for the address of the person who the dynamite was for and I remembered that Mr. Overell said that he did not want anyone to know about it so I gave an address, I believe it was address in Palmdale and he asked me to sign the name of the person I was buying the dynamite for in my own name and because Mr. Overell did not want to be connected with it, I decided I did not want to be connected with it either so I gave him two names, I don't know where they came from, I just thought them up and wrote them on the receipt.

Q And did Mr. Hill give you a copy of the receipt at that time?

A He did.

Q Now directing your attention to People's Exhibit #113 in evidence in this case which purports to be a receipt of the Trojan Powder Company, I will ask you if you recognize that as a copy of the receipt that was give you by Mr. Hill at that time.

A I believe it is.

Q And subsequent to you having given the receipt to Louise and its being put in the glove compartment of the car what happened next?

A Mr. Hill came around to the other side of the car and got in and directed me to drive down a short dirt road and up a hill where the magazine shed was, and he went in and brought out a wooden box and gave it to me and I put it in the turtleback of the automobile and the he said that he would walk on down to the location of the hill and I drove down there and he walked down and he handed me a cardboard box by a stone shed down there and he said that those were caps and I asked Louise if she would get the money out of the glove compartment.

Q What was done with the caps?

A They were put in the back seat.

Q The back seat of the car and the wooden box was put in the turtleback of the car, is that correct?

A That is correct.

Q Go ahead about the payment of the money.

A And then Louise handed him some silver dollars that I had in the glove compartment and I got in the car and we left.

Q And how long were you at Chatsworth on that occasion?

A I would say about a half an hour.

———

The prosecution's cross examination of Bud was vanilla. They seemed to be more concerned with preserving their theory of motive than disproving the defense claim that Walter Overell either committed suicide or by accidentally blowing up the boat. It's possible that they saw that theory as so preposterous that they felt it unnecessary to give it legs by acknowledging it. As a matter of fact, it was preposterous but the jury bought it, or at least used it as a crutch to support their emotion-based verdict. They could have brought out that Bud claimed he told Hill he did not know why the man for whom he was buying the dynamite wanted it but on the receipt he said it was for mining.

They could have asked Bud if he did not think it strange that a man totally unfamiliar with explosives would know to ask for "caps." Walter Overell had not been in the military. He had started in the furniture business, and made his money in finance. He would not likely know the jargon for fuses. They could have easily proved that Bud had been to the Chatsworth area before and would not need a map. The map of choice in those days was the Thomas

Brothers map and you looked up addresses by the street name not the city.
No effort was made to cross him up.

Cross examination of Gollum.

Here is a small sample of the state cross examination of George Rector Gollum:

Q Mr. Gollum, I take it from the gist of your testimony any rate that at all times since July 13, 1946, you have been deeply in love with your co-defendant, Miss Overell.

A That is correct.

Q And that was true at the time of your arrest and following your arrest?

A That is correct.

Q You were aware were you not that on March 20, at the time that you first discussed the matter of the boat having been dynamited with Sheriff Musick and Mr. McGaff that Miss Overell was in jail charged with the murder of her parents?

A I was aware of that.

Q You were also at that time claiming it to be a fact, were you not, that Mr. Overell had procured you to purchase dynamite and that you had turned the dynamite over to him.

A Yes.

Q You did not state to Mr. Musick or Mr. McGaff the circumstances of your having purchased dynamite for Mr. Overell, did you?

A I did not.

Q In fact you stated that you did not purchase any dynamite at any time or any place.

A That is correct.

Q And that was not true at the time you said it, was it.

A It was not.

Q And you knew it was not true.

A I did.

Q And you knew at that time that your co-defendant, Miss Overell was in jail charged with murder.

A I did.

Q Will you explain to this jury why you did not tell the truth to these officers at that time in response to this matter?

A I had been advised by Mr. Beirne not to talk about the case about the time the conversation about the dynamite took place. That is why I did not.

Q And that is the only reason is it?

Q Now I think you have stated that, on the night before the death of Mr. and Mrs. Overell, I mean on Friday night, you ate a lot of what you call rose vanilla ice cream.

A. That is correct.

Q Did that have any effect on your system?

A No more than ice cream usually does.

Q What I meant to say was it did not make you sick or ill?

A It did not.

Q It doesn't account for the fact that after you left the boat on the night of the 15th of March that you were unable to eat?

Objection by Mr. Beirne, over ruled by Judge Morrison

A I was able to eat sir.

Q How much did you eat?

A I ate a half of one hamburger.

Q And you ate no more?

A I did not.

Q You hadn't anything to eat since approximately noon of that day?

A That was correct.

Q And normally you have a healthy appetite?

A I do.

Q Is it not a fact that you were unable to eat or the fact that you appetite was not as good as usual caused by the fact that you had just killed Mr. and Mrs. Overell?

A No sir it was caused by the fact that I was tired and I did not particularly like the quality of the hamburger.

Q So you fed it to Miss Overell?

A I did not feed it to her, she asked me for it.

———

Mr. Williams cross examination is almost laughable. The question of why he originally lied to investigators about buying the dynamite was an excellent question but there was no follow up. He could have challenged some of his answers. He could have delved more into Gollum's account of Mr. Overell asking him to buy the dynamite, for example, "Why would he trust you, when he did not want you in the family?" Instead, he moves into the inane line about the ice cream and Bud's appetite. Softball questions that Bud hit over the fence and made him more sympathetic than the prosecuting attorney.

More Gollum Cross Examination:

Q When you left the Mary E, or rather when you left the vicinity of the Mary E to take Miss Overell home that night, I think you testified that you stopped at your parent's home.

A I did.

Q And you went in and Miss Overell stayed outside.

A She did.

Q And did you tell your mother what happened?

A I did.

Q And did your mother come out then?

A She did not.

Q And was there any suggestion made of taking Miss Overell to the home of one or the other Uncles?

A There was.

Q And who was it that was opposed to that?

A Louise said that "she wanted to go home.

Q Did you make any effort to secure a chaperone for her that night?

A When I called up her grandmother's and told the maid that we were alone and she said that she would call the uncle, I presumed she meant right away and she would be up right away.

Q And the result was, you did stay alone that night.

A We did.

Q Now following that night, and on the next morning, I think you testified that you and Louise did play ping pong.

A We did.

Q And you also testified that you laughed and joked around the house that day.

A We did.

Q And was the same thing true the following day, on Monday?

A Not to such an extent, no sir.

Q And did you on the following Monday go down and do some shopping?

A Monday evening, we shopped on the way home.

Q And what did you buy?

A Groceries.

Q Did you not buy some phonograph records?

A No sir.

Q Did you buy some phonograph records on Monday?

A We did not.

Q Did you buy phonograph records on Tuesday?

A We did not.

Q You have seen the phonograph records that were produced here in court?

A I have.

Q Where were those phonograph records obtained?

A The Village Music Center on the corner of Wilshire and Western.

Q And when did you buy those?

A They were purchased about the 3rd of March, I believe.

Q They were not purchased on a day or two following the death of Miss Overell's parents?

A No sir, they were not. Louise gave them to me for a birthday present.

Q And they were at the Flintridge home following the death of her parents, were they not?

A They were?

Q When were they taken to the Flintridge home?

A They were in the automobile, my automobile when I emptied it out on Tuesday night.

—————

Mr. Williams did a good job bringing out the incomprehensibly blithe attitude of the couple – particularly on the part of Miss Overell. The problem here is that all it proved was that perhaps Miss Overell did not love or miss her parents which could be the result of many causes. He should have stopped here. The point was made. He undoubtedly had bad information regarding the purchase of phonograph records. Gollum would not lie about that, it would have been too easy to disprove. The net effect was to lend credence to the later accusation by the defense that the state was abusing, hiding or falsifying evidence.

The defense was brutal and effective. They attacked every witness the state presented. They discredited Dr. Montanus, the physician appointed to conduct the second autopsy, by making him admit that he couldn't precisely state how long it took for rigor mortise to set in. They also made rigor mortise an issue with Charles Baltz, the mortician. Rigor mortise was never a factor in the case. They brought in experts to prove where the explosion would have put the bodies. This was irrelevant. The bodies had been floated by the flooding water and no one knew where they would have been otherwise.

The two defenses worked together but not in complete harmony. From the beginning, Jacobs wanted separate trials, Kaufman did not. Kaufman felt that Gollum's best chance was riding on the coat tails of Miss Overell. Jacobs was somewhat constrained in his efforts by Louise's loyalty to Gollum whose spell she was under. At the beginning, their chances looked bleak. Late in the trial, after the total alienation of Bud and Louise, Jacobs made a motion to sever all the evidence against Bud from application to Louise. In effect this was another attempt to make separate trials, after the fact. With the conspiracy, evidence against one is evidence against both. There was no evidence beyond Bud's testimony that linked Louise to the explosives.

They challenged the blood grouping of the Overells. Ray Pinker, of the Los Angeles Police Department Crime Lab, a chemist, testified that the blood on Gollum's clothing was the same blood type as Walter Overell. They mercilessly and unfairly attacked Captain McGaff's handling of the evidence.

Perhaps their most outrageous move was to spend two days on their cross examination of the state's handwriting expert who identified the signatures on the receipt for the explosives even though they had Gollum admit that he bought the explosives. Their plan was sheer genius and represented the only chance Gollum and Overell had. They intended, not only to make the police and prosecution look inept, but to look corrupt. The first part is honorable the second part is not and is pervasive in the criminal justice system. So spending all that time on disproving something they would later admit, was just part of their plan to try the prosecution and shift the focus from the defendants to the state.

A closing argument was made for Gollum by Kaufman and Overell by Jacobs. Together, they used 400 pages of transcripts.

JACOB'S CLOSING ARGUMENT FOR OVERELL.

Following is the last part of Jacob's closing argument for Louis Overell"

> Let them talk of Dr. Mathes[9] and stand up before you as an honest and fair prosecutor and say "Dr. Mathes on page so and so, he testified that...." Now, ladies and gentlemen they will further say "that's uncontradicted, that's honest fair testimony of an honorable upright medical man," and then let them take the testimony of mortician Baltz. I would love to have permission to take the Baltz testimony and write it up and take it into the jury room and have them read it. It's too bad we can't do that.

> They are relying, ladies and gentlemen, on Mortician Baltz to establish beyond a reasonable doubt and to a moral certainty that Mrs. Overell was dead four, a minimum, that's what he said, a minimum of four hours and a maximum of six hours at the time she was taken over to the mortician's place of business. What testimony. When you get him on cross examination and you ask him certain questions. "And can you tell me, Mr. Baltz, when rigor mortise can set in within a half hour?" "No." But he is willing to help out the prosecution and tell you the minimum time

---

9 Dr. Mathes performed the first of the two autopsies.

of death of Mrs. Overell was four hours and the maximum time was six hours and he also…well I can remember it without the transcript, I was going to give you the book and page, but that wouldn't help you any, he also testified that a variation, and he tries to doctor that up a half a dozen times, but finally he down and admitted that a variation from his time was anywhere from an hour and an hour and a half. Either way he got that far and then he was asked again about rigor mortise and if he could tell what time it had set in and he said, "no, I can't answer that" but he is still willing to help out the prosecution "a minimum of four hours and a maximum of six hours because that fits in with the run of things. Is that testimony true testimony? Is that the kind of testimony you ladies and gentlemen want to convict that girl on. Do you want to take away her life and liberty on the testimony of Baltz and Mathes and Montanus? Do you want to take her life and liberty away by reason of her actions and her conduct? She has been criticized concerning things she shouldn't be regardless of her actions or her sweethearts. What do you suppose would have happened to your child or my child if she or he had been sent to jail charged with this terrible charge of murder and with photographers flying around and talking to her and taking pictures asking her to do this and asking her to do that making fun so she would laugh and then writing up a nice piece in the paper? Get her to move this way and move that way and have her go over there and then over here so Adele Rogers St. John could take her apart. Wonderful. And then the prosecution says to you her actions and conduct should be considered by you and the way she did after the tragedy and her actions and conduct now.

Heaven help me ladies and gentlemen if these kinds of things are going to cause you to convict an innocent girl just because a representative of the state of California has been sent down, a great prosecutor, to convict her, but I don't think you're going to do that.

─────

Kaufman closing arugument for Gollum.

The last part of Kaufman's closing argument:

> *Louise's heart is broken. She is all alone. The state wants to punish her even more by sending her to prison and Bud to the gas chamber. This is murder or nothing and without compromise. There is no distinction between the gas chamber and life. A guilty person would not walk up to a police chief's desk and give him a camera with damaging evidence inside. I don't believe Bud put the receipt for the dynamite inside. I don't think Walter Overell did either. I believe Walter Overell left the dynamite receipt in the desk at his home. Investigators found it there and planted it in the camera. I think the whole thing was staged. I think Tom McGaff knew what he was going to find when he opened the camera. If McGaff had taken Overell's fingerprints, he would have found them on the camera.*
>
> *There has been a lot of criticism of Louise for returning to her home after the explosion. When someone dies in the family, it is just a natural impulse to want to go home. It is not displaying a guilty conscience when you go home. Louise lost everything when that boat exploded. Her other relatives show that. They get on the stand and testify against her. They write notes to the prosecution like they did this morning—you saw them. Oh, once in a while they approached her and put their hand on her shoulder. Most of the time, they just sit there, though.*

Verdict.

Judge Morrison gave the jury instructions on the afternoon of Friday, October 3, 1947. The jury deliberated for 48 hours. There were four ballots cast. The first one was 7-5 for acquittal. It was whittled down to 11-1 on Saturday night and the one remaining holdout was bullied into voting for acquittal.

Hundreds of people were waiting in and outside the courtroom and erupted into cheers when they heard the verdict. It was a great day for jurisprudence. Otto Jacobs and the dream team succeeded in an uphill battle to free two brutal murderers, proving once again to the world that in our balanced adversarial system, a guilty person has a 50/50 chance of being acquitted. Louise is shown after the verdict, indicating she is as free as a bird.

Bud and Louise were not the first people to get away with murder and they weren't the last. It will go on. Without going into the spiritual element, it would appear that Bud and Louise did not really "get away with murder;" maybe temporarily but their life after the murders says otherwise. The couple was free but neither lived happily ever after.

Part III

JUSTICE DENIED

The Overell Gollum not guilty verdict is one of the most outrageous miscarriages of justice in the last 100 years; at least among high profile cases. In researching controversial high profile cases involving a not guilty verdict, only four stand out that are comparable; the trials of Lizzie Borden for murdering her parents with an axe in eighteen92, O.J. Simpson, Robert Blake and Casey Anthony. The author followed OJ trial daily on television and the Overell murder trial in the papers and on the radio as a boy in 1947.

There is no rational explanation for the O.J. decision. As in the Overell decision, it boils down to more effective lawyering. The defense attacked *every* prosecution witness and item of evidence; usually unfairly and illogically but effective in confusing the jurors or giving them a "reason" to substantiate an intangible bias. The public sentiment and press coverage pointed to a conviction in all four cases; less in the Overell and Simpson cases. Marcia Clarke, one of the prosecuting attorneys in the Simpson Case, and an outstanding trial lawyer make some points in her analysis of the Anthony jury that are clearly germane to the Overell jury:

> *"And so, every bit of evidence presented by the prosecution could've been tinged with doubt. At the end of the day, the jury might have found that they just couldn't convict her based on evidence that was reconcilable*

with an innocent explanation—even if the weight of logic favored the guilty one.

"Jury instructions are so numerous and complex, it's a wonder jurors ever wade through them. And so it should come as no surprise that they can sometimes get stuck along the way. The instruction on circumstantial evidence is confusing even to lawyers. And reasonable doubt? That's the hardest, most elusive one of all. And I think it's where even the most fair-minded jurors can get derailed.

"How? By confusing <u>reasonable doubt</u> with a <u>reason to</u> doubt. Some believe that thinking was in play in the Simpson case. After the verdict was read in the Simpson case, as the jury was leaving, one of them, I was later told, said: "We think he probably did it. We just did not think they proved it beyond a reasonable doubt." In every case, a defense attorney will do his or her best to give the jury a reason to doubt. "Some other dude did it," or "some other dude threatened him." But those reasons don't necessarily equate with a reasonable doubt. A reason does not equal reasonable. Sometimes, that distinction can get lost."[10]

The Overell jury doesn't deserve the latitude or assumption of fair minded-ness that Miss Clarke gives the other two juries. Miss Clarke also distinguishes between "<u>reasonable doubt</u>" and "<u>reason to doubt</u>." A more accurate distinction, at least in the case of the Overell jury would be "reasonable doubt" vs. "<u>unreasonable doubt</u>."

The evidence is overwhelming. Gollum bought the dynamite. This was not disputed after he was caught with receipt. The defense claim that it was bought for and at the request of Walter Overell is preposterous.

1. If he were going to blow up his own boat…for any reason, Gollum would be the last person he would ask to buy it. The fact is, he would buy it himself so no one would know that he had purchased dynamite just before his boat blew up. Surely he wouldn't trust Bud with that kind of incriminating information.

---

10 http://news.yahoo.com/worse-o-j-231200719.html

2. There is no plausible reason that he would want to blow up the boat. The Overells loved the boat. They loved the water. The assertion that he was in financial trouble and had paid more for the boat than it was worth is inconsistent with his proven acumen as a business man. The implication that he needed money badly enough to defraud the insurance company was inconsistent with his character. Walter Overell was simply not dishonest. When his estate was evaluated after his death, the net worth was $310,000. In today's dollar, that is equivalent to over $2 Million. Additionally, the economy in 1947 was excellent and Walter Overell was in a position to make a lot more money.

3. Suicide is out of the question for the reasons stated above and he wouldn't have done it with his wife aboard.

4. If Gollum had asked him at noon on Friday with no time limit, why would he feel compelled to drop everything and do it immediately; especially on a Friday afternoon. It's hardly likely, if Overell was going to blow up his boat, that he would be having all the work done on it. If it were a bad investment, why would he pour more money in it at that time? Why would he be smuggling the dynamite aboard that day when his wife, daughter, daughter's boyfriend and two mechanics were going to be on and off the boat all day and on a day that he was going to move it into a boat repair dock?

Assuming that Overell asked Gollum to buy dynamite for him on Friday the 14th, it's not reasonable that he would take it aboard the Mary E the next day. It's not reasonable that he would want to blow up the boat or even putter around with the dynamite and caps on the 15th with all the other people and activity, activity which involved a lot of unpredictable movement, happening on the same day. That could only be used as a basis for "unreasonable doubt." It could not possibly have happened that way.

Without the possibility or likelihood that Overell was responsible for the explosion, the only other alternative is that someone else killed the Overells either by the explosion or by beating them to death and blowing up the boat to make it look like an accident. This, of course, is the state's contention. It is the only logical, or even possible, explanation. Why, then, did they fail? Before the trial began, the consensus was, at least as expressed by the media, was that it was an open and shut case, or to use the modern metaphor, a "slam dunk." It is the author's opinion that the prosecution was simply out lawyered. It's a sad fact that adversarial based justice systems have developed over time so that on a level playing field, a guilty person has a 50/50 chance of being acquitted. Given money and celebrity status, the field is tilted toward acquittal. In other cases, the field is tilted toward conviction. In this case, the Overell murder case in the Old Orange County Court House in 1947, the playing field was level. The defense lawyers were just better than the prosecution lawyers.

To simplify it, Otto Jacobs was better than Eugene Williams. At the time of the trial Otto Jacobs had never lost a capital case. His strategy was pure genius.

1. Make the cops and prosecutors look inept and/or dishonest.

2. Give them an alternative theory.

3. Make the defendants more sympathetic figures than the cops or prosecutors.

4. Confuse the jurors.

In the adversarial system, the objective is to win. Truth becomes irrelevant. Both sides try to suppress evidence. In this case the defense had no evidence other than the testimony of Bud and Louise. Bud claimed Walter told him to buy the dynamite and that the Overells liked him. Louise claimed that her family accepted Bud. There was no corroboration. Even Bud's claim that Overell asked him to buy the explosives was not corroborated by Louise.

The defense was saved from making a big mistake in severing the trial by the prosecutions resistance to it. The state made a huge mistake by not asking for it. Hind sight is better than fore sight but there is a probability that they could have convinced Louise to testify against Bud and at least get one conviction. Understandably, they thought they could get two. They wanted both.

Trial attorneys are not under oath when they make statements in court. Although they accuse cops and witnesses of lying, they actually *do* lie; and with impunity. Neither are they inhibited by the potential of law suits for libel. They make libelous statements. In the Simpson case, Johnny Cochrane accused the cops/prosecution in a generic sense, and that was reprehensible, but in the Overell case, it got personal. Otto Jacobs implied that Charles Baltz, the mortician who embalmed the bodies, was lying but S. B. Kaufman, Gollum's attorney, accused Sheriff Musick, Chief Hodgkinson and Captain Thomas McGaff of planting evidence. This was a lie and he must have known it was a lie. Unfortunately, in our system, this is permitted; even encouraged by the emphasis we place, through our pricing system, on winning.

In his closing argument, Kaufman accused Captain McGaff of finding the receipt for the dynamite, bearing a signature falsified by Gollum, in Walter Overell's desk and placing it in Overell's camera. He then asks the hypothetical question, "Would a guilty person knowingly carry a camera to the desk of the chief of police and hand it to him?" A better question would be "Why would McGaff put it in the camera and hope that Gollum would carry it with him when he went to the police department?" Why wouldn't he put it in Gollum's car or in the pocket of his clothing in their possession? The answer, of course, is that he would but he did neither. A jury looking for "reasonable cause," would ask this question. A jury accepting "unreasonable cause" would not.

Otto Jacobs was not quite so bad by only implying that Dr. Lawrence Mathes and Dr. John J. Montanus and Charles Baltz, the mortician, were lying. The two doctors had both examined the bodies at the direction of the Deputy Coroner. They agreed that death was a result of head trauma that occurred before the explosion. Baltz was called to estimate the time of death. It was probably a mistake. He did not do a very good job as a witness and the exact time was not important. The critical factor was that they were dead before the explosion. Baltz testimony was not a factor. His estimate of time of death was between 4 and six hours. Jacobs made him look foolish by forcing to admit that it was not precise. Precision was not needed. He made him look more foolish by asking him the extraneous question about rigor mortise – how long it takes to set in. The normal time is about 3 hours but Baltz couldn't narrow it down because of other factors involved in Post Mortem Interval, or PMI. This information from the Forensic Medicine is something that the jury should have been told at the time that Jacobs was embarrassing Baltz for not being able to precisely estimate when rigor mortise would set in:

Both the time of death and the postmortem interval cannot be determined with 100% accuracy, particularly when a body is found in advanced state of decomposition or is recovered from fire, water, or ice. Therefore, time of death and PMI are given as estimates, and can vary from hours to days, or from months to years, depending on each particular case.[11]

11 http://www.enotes.com/forensic-science/time-death

It's not the responsibility, under the adversarial system of criminal justice for attorneys to provide the jury with fact or real information; it is their responsibility to make them vote not guilty for their clients. If it takes misinformation or even lies to do this, it's all part of the so-called even playing field. Unfortunately, the prosecution is compelled to show the defense all the evidence they have and are punished if they withhold exculpatory evidence. The same is not true for defense attorneys withholding evidence of guilt.

The problem the prosecution had in this case was the incredulity of the murders. It is hard to fathom how this couple who had, if not everything certainly enough, could commit such a brutal and unlikely murder. A look into their history is revealing.

Part IV

A PERFECT STORM

I n the summer 1935 Mr. and Mrs. George Rector, Bud Gollum's grand-parents, were entertaining on their yacht in Catalina. Bud's parents, Fred and Wilhelmina Gollum, Walter E. and Beulah Overell, along with a few others, were present.

This was the first time that the ill-fated couple, Louise Overell and Bud Gollum met. Nine year old Bud rowed the Overell family out to the yacht. Louise, a pudgy little girl, was annoyed at Bud's pompous and condescending attitude but she thought he was cute. Bud, intent on impressing the adults with his maturity and rowing skill, ignored her. Bud was a socially awkward kid and preferred being around adults than kids his own age. All his life he would have trouble making and keeping friends. He would become some-what of a pseudo-intellectual and worked at making people think he was intelligent; some were impressed, most were not. Actually, he was, at best, average. He was doted on by his mother but his father was aloof and soon was divorced by his mother, Wilhelmina, who married Dr. Joseph Stomel. Dr. Stomel was not interested in a fatherly relationship with Bud and his one year older sister Wilafred.

Bud's father, Fred, was a fairly successful stock broker and Bud grew up comfortably as far as wealth was concerned. He and Wilafred attended 3rd Street Elementary School, John Brown Junior High and graduated from Los Angeles High School. Those years were uneventful. His primary social activity was in the Boy Scouts. Bud has been referred to as a loner by journalists covering his murder trial years later. A loner can be described simply as a person who does not actively seek human interaction or prefers to be alone.

> *"Some individuals see their status as a loner as beneficial. They may feel they can view things reflectively, mature much faster, seek knowledge, reach their goals more easily, and be more focused on the task at hand. Disconnected from the people around them, they are more likely to make their own decisions and avoid peer pressure. Some individuals refuse to interact with others because of perceived or actual superiority in terms of ethics or intellect. They relate only to individuals they consider worthy of their time and attention. Therefore, this type of loner will have very few intimate relationships. Loners may socialize greatly with those in whom they can confide. It can take a while for this bond to occur. If someone unknown to a loner enters the social group, the loner may automatically shell up.*
>
> *Shy or lacking self-esteem, some loners can socialize only with people they see constantly. This is in part because many are overly self-conscious and believe people are constantly sizing up their attributes. Insecure loners find it excruciating to be in the physical presence of others because they worry they will be judged negatively. Anxiety is a common feature of their social interactions. Self-hatred is sometimes the underlying motivation for why a person may isolate him or herself. A sense of alienation from society can develop as a result—even though it is self-imposed."* [12]

Beulah Louise Overell was born when her mother was 39 years old. It's doubtful that she was planned. Obviously, or at least it would seem so, the Overells did not want children; being very much caught up in the social life of the upper class. Newspaper accounts called her a cool character. Some of her friends referred to her as stone-faced. The transcripts of her testimony at trial would indicate a high degree of intelligence and unflappability. The exchange of letters during their incarceration would indicate that she was more intelligent than Bud but more malleable and, initially, definitely under his spell.

---

12 http://en.wikipedia.org/wiki/Loner

The Overells/Jungquist, Gollum/Rectors were intertwined socially. Louise's mother Beulah and Bud's mother Wilhelmina were friends before each was married, having attended church together at the Wilshire Christian Church.

In the summer of 1945, the Rectors, Bud's grandparents, were entertaining the Overells along with Beulah's brother Emmanuel Jungquist and his daughter Marjorie; perhaps other family members. The subject of Bud, who was in the Navy, came up. Bud's family was worried about Bud; particularly his social life. He had joined the Navy directly out of high school and was somewhat socially backward. He had no close friends. His mother, Wilhelmina, was concerned as well. She had divorced his father and Bud had no real father figure in his life. From his infrequent letters, it was obvious that he was not enjoying being in the Navy. Bud's Grandmother suggested that it would be nice if Louise and her cousin Marjorie would write him a letter. Louise was less than enthusiastic, remembering her somewhat negative impression she had of him when she first met him when she was only six years old. Beulah agreed with Mrs. Rector, thinking that it might be a good idea for Louise to have some kind of relationship with a boy. Louise was worried about rejection; that had been the most common reaction by boys in the past. She was homely, smart mouthed and probably brighter than most boys her age. Her sharp tongue became her coping mechanism. Marjorie never wrote him but Louise did.

Louise was an unloved but over indulged teenager. She had a governess/teacher and attended private schools. She loved clothes but had poor taste in what she wore, not having the normal attention and guidance from her mother. Beulah had been strikingly attractive in her youth and received more that her share of attention from men in the upper social activities. Beulah was only 39 years old when Louise was conceived and still had an appealing figure. She was resentful of what an unwanted pregnancy could do to her figure. There is no evidence of promiscuity by Beulah but an unwanted pregnancy is more likely to occur in the careless passion of an affair than in the more perfunctory and routine sex of a marriage. Louise inherited none of her parents' physical attractiveness which leaves open the possibility of outside genes.

For whatever reason, Louise reluctantly agreed to write Bud, sure of the usual rejection. She first wrote him in November when he was in the Philippine Islands. Bud replied and a steady correspondence began and continued until he was discharged. Pictures were exchanged and the letters took on a subtle sexual undertone as they got to know each other better. Louise was not attractive but buxom and was excited at the first interest displayed by a potential boyfriend. She had a normal, maybe even elevated sex drive. Bud was inexperienced with women; his only sexual contact being with prostitutes.

He was aware of the Overell's wealth. He grew up surrounded by wealth but not quite in possession. The 1930 census shows his father renting a house that was valued at $20,000 which would be a very expensive home for that time. When his mother remarried Dr. Joseph Stomel they moved to 2301 Carmona Avenue with his five children from a previous marriage. Louise' Grandmother Jungquist lived at 504 S. Manhattan Place which in 1947 was in an exclusive area. The home has since been converted or torn down and rebuilt as an apartment house. Bud's grandparents, the George Rectors, lived one block away from Louise's grandmother at 406 S. Manhattan Place and, as mentioned earlier, Bud's mother and Louise's mother attended the same church. The Overells lived in a palatial home at 607 Los Robles, Flintridge, and Bud was familiar with the home. Contemporary accounts of the trial state that Bud was a Pre-med student but he was enrolled at Los Angeles City College which most likely did not have a program designated specifically as Pre-med. Bud told people that he was Pre-med to impress them and to please his stepfather who was a doctor. At this stage of his life, he had no intention of working for a living. When he was discharged from the Navy in June of 1946, he had never held a job. He planned to keep it that way.

Soon after his discharge Bud went to see Louise in May of 1946 just before his discharge, while she was at her grandmother's house, and the romance took off. They started going together in July and became engaged on the 13th of July, 1946. Neither had any experience in a romantic relationship. Louise was a virgin and Bud's experience was casual sex with prostitutes while in the Navy. Both tended to be lascivious, particularly Bud. As he was her teacher, as it were, she adapted his attitude. Bud was, without a doubt, primarily interested in her because of her wealth but being inexperienced was swept away with raw sexual desire. Their sexual pleasure was mutual, frequent and coarse.

As they found out about the involvement of their daughter, the Overell's resisted. They never tried to break the couple up but absolutely refused to approve of the marriage. They tolerated Bud because of the longtime friendship between the Rectors and Jungquists, but they never really liked him. Not many people did. They were suspicious of his motives. They were painfully aware of their daughter's lack of charm and beauty – or even comeliness. They were also painfully aware of Bud's total lack of social skills and wouldn't have objected to his materialistic motives were it not for the fact that they just did not want him in the family. Sadly, Louise's feelings were secondary. They always considered her an encumbrance to their lifestyle. Louise was painfully aware of their lack of warmth and of their unacknowledged resentment of her intrusion in their life. Louise, as well as Bud, demonstrated many elements of anti-social behavior. It's difficult to determine how much her cool parental relationship contributed:

Antisocial individuals can suffer emotional pain for a variety of reasons. Like anyone else, antisocial individuals have a deep wish to be loved and cared for. This desire remains frequently unfulfilled, however, as it is obviously not easy for another person to get close to someone with such repellent personality characteristics. Antisocial individuals are at least periodically aware of the effects of their behavior on others and can be genuinely saddened by their inability to control it. The lives of most antisocial individuals are devoid of a stable social network or warm, close bonds.

The life histories of antisocial individuals are often characterized by a chaotic family life, lack of parental attention and guidance, parental substance abuse and antisocial behavior, poor relationships, divorce, and adverse neighborhoods. They may feel that they are prisoners of their own etiological determination and believe that they had, in comparison with normal people, fewer opportunities or advantages in life.

Despite their outward arrogance, antisocial individuals, inside, feel inferior to others and know they are stigmatized by their own behavior. Although some antisocial individuals are superficially adapted to their environment and are even popular, they feel they must carefully hide their true nature because it will not be accepted by others. This leaves antisocial individuals with a difficult choice: adapt and participate in an empty, unreal life, or do not adapt and live a lonely life isolated from the social community. They see the love and friendship others share and feel dejected knowing they will never take part in it.[13]

While Bud's attraction and attachment to Louise was complex, mixing shallow sordid love with selfish greed, Louise saw Bud as a savior who would salvage a life that she had already, at the tender age of 17, accepted would be without love or normal social interaction. It was OK with her if this new life was limited to his world. She gave him the nick name of Pops because he was, in her mind, taking the place of her father as well as being her lover.

Their lives began to revolve around their sexual encounters which involved a wide range of activity including that which is considered perverted by most. There is no need to go into detail but the letters exchanged during their pretrial incarceration which were read in the trial and later ordered burned by Judge Morrison, tell the story. Their behavior was referenced in the state's attorney's opening remarks. They were so explicit that they had to be redacted in the Los Angeles Examiner newspaper replicas of the letters.

Their appeals to Walter and Beulah for approval were more and more confrontational and continued to be rejected. Bud initially presented their case but Louise, who was not used to not having her way, took over the campaign.

"Mother," Louise said, "I just don't understand what you have against Bud. You know his family, you are friends with his mother and you are the one who encouraged the relationship by encouraging me to write to him. Now, I'm in love with him and you don't approve."

"You are both too young and you have no idea what love is."

"Mother, I am nearly eighteen years old, I know my feelings and I haven't exactly been surrounded with boys seeking my attention. Bud loves me!"

"Bud loves your money," Beulah replied sardonically.

"Thank you for your vote of confidence, mother. I know it's difficult for you to believe anyone could love me since you don't."

---

13 http://www.myaspergerschild.com/2009/10/antisocial-behavior-in-aspergers-teens.html

"Don't you be disrespectful to me, young lady," Beulah shouted as Louise stormed out of the room.

Later on, Bud called Walter to set up an appointment to talk to him. Walter agreed without enthusiasm, knowing full well why he wanted the meeting. The young couple had spent a lot of time with her parents during the season and Bud thought the timing was as good as it was going to get.

Louise answered the door and let Bud into the house and called, "Father, Bud is here and wants to talk to you."

"Hello, Bud, let's go into my study."

"Louise, you wait in here," Walter says as she is following them into the study. "This is between Bud and me."

Without changing expression, Louise petulantly replies to her father, "This involves me and I resent not being present."

Walter is obviously annoyed but before he can reply Bud motions to her with his hands to calm down and says, "I called your father to ask him to speak with me and he was kind enough to agree. I think it will be fine." Walter, a strong personality type is visibly annoyed at Bud's audacity in stepping between him and his discipline with his daughter. The Overells, both Walter and Beulah, are at once, resentful and possessive of Louise. He hesitates briefly and motions for Bud to follow him into the office and for Louise to stay. Louise is fuming but doesn't change expression and stands and stares as they shut the door. Louise is becoming more and more resentful of her parents. She had, since her childhood days, ceased loving them or expecting their affection.

Walter's office is huge and completely paneled in dark stained oak and lined with book cases. Walter sat down at his huge desk and motioned for Bud to sit down. The scene is deliberately set to give the appearance more of job interview than one of a young man asking for his daughters hand in marriage. Walter is not likely to grant either to Bud. Once seated, Bud nervously put his hands on the table and blurted out, "Mr. Overell, I'm in love with Louise and want to marry her."

Walter has learned to not expect much from Bud in the way of eloquence but is surprised at Bud's clumsy approach.

"Well, Bud," Walter begins, "I knew you were growing close but I had no idea that you were at this stage," he continues somewhat disingenuously. "I assume you are talking about the future when you are out of school and ready to take care of her, she has some very expensive habits."

"No, Mr. Overell, we want to get married right now before we finish school."

"How do you expect to live?"

Bud is surprised at the question having expected a direct rejection as Louise got from her mother. "I have the GI Bill to pay for my schooling," Bud stammers, "and we can live with my parents."

"Have you discussed this with your parents?"

"They know we intend to get married."

"Do they know you intend to live with them when you are married?"

"I am sure they wouldn't mind."

"But you haven't asked!"

"No."

"Well, Bud, you have my permission to date my daughter and even to be engaged to her but I can't approve of marriage until you are in a position to support her…and yourself."

Bud is frustrated and silently enraged. He sat for a few seconds trying to think of a rebuttal but could think of nothing else to say. He slowly arose from his chair, clumsily thanked Walter for the meeting and left the room. He was greeted by Louise as he left the room and they went outside. When sure that he could not be overhead, Bud said, "The son of a bitch said no!" Louise was not surprised but shared his anger.

The two of them left together in Bud's car and went to his room to plan and to have sex. After their lust was assuaged, and their anger abated, they returned to planning. One characteristic they shared was stubborn determination. Louise was simply not used to not getting her way. She suggested that Bud enlist the aid of his mother, Wilhelmina, in trying to influence Beulah. The two of them had been friends, or at least acquainted for over 20 years. Actually, the friendship between the two families was engendered more through Grandmother Jungquist and the George Rectors who had been neighbors.

Several days later, Bud and Louise met with Grandmother Jungquist, Beulah Overell's mother, at her home on S. Manhattan place and expressed their desire to get married and their frustration with the resistance of Louise's parents. Grandmother Jungquist, also named Louise, was in favor of the relationship from the beginning. In her wisdom, she recognized the flaws in both the young people and believed it was the best thing that could happen to both of them. They also appealed to Bud's mother, Wilhelmina for support. She also approved of the match but was cool to the idea of getting involved, not being that confident in her ability to influence Beulah. These meetings took place around the end of July and early August of 1946. At Bud and Louise's insistence, Bud's mother and Louise's mother agreed to intervene on their behalf with Walter and Beulah.

On August 24th at Walter's birthday party at the Flintridge home, the families, including Louise Jungquist, Bud's mother, Louise's uncle Emmanuel and perhaps the Rectors, met with the young couple not present, to discuss the marriage. It was a long meeting, nearly an hour, without rancor or any display of animosity. The outcome was general approval of the relationship and agreement that they should wait until Bud was through school. Walter and Beulah actually did not want Bud in the family but rather than openly express their disapproval of Bud went along with the idea assuming that four years of seeing Bud would be more than Louise needed to see through him. They both recognized that Bud's primary motive was her money but saw no point in intervening in the relationship at this point. All involved surely were aware that the relationship had become intimate and the possibility of a pregnancy created differently perceived implications for those involved. Walter and Beulah, obviously, feared it the most but saw no way of forbidding any contact. They just did not have that kind of control over their daughter.

Bud's family and Louise Jungquist naively thought that the two families' approval of the marriage, albeit at a much later date, would satisfy the young couple and when Louise's Grandmother Jungquist along with Bud's mother apprised them of the result of the meeting they were not prepared for the rage they displayed. Bud was particularly outspoken and profane in his anger at Walter and Beulah. Louise was always softer spoken and more intelligent than Bud but by now was completely under his spell. He had initiated her sexually, had introduced her to lust and prurient pleasure that she enjoyed to the fullest and was afraid of losing. She was not too sure that Bud's interest in her family fortune was not a primary motivating factor but she refused to think of it. If the money was what it took, so be it; she had limited options and she knew it.

Bud told the family that absent her parents' consent, they would be married without it on April 30, 1947, her eighteen[th] birthday. The Overells countered with the promise to cut Louise off from her inheritance if they did. The game of chicken had begun. Different members of the two families silently took sides but there were no clear schisms. Bud and Louise's engagement and their relationship continued with an uneasy non articulated truce. Bud continued to be welcome in the Overell home and was invited, along with Louise to events involving Walter's associations.

In spite of the rift over the marriage, life within and between the two families went on, ostensibly, with no problems. Bud and Louise continued to see each other in the presence of the families but their resentment smoldered beneath the surface and was developing into a deadly hatred. Louise, who had never been close to her parents and who had always gotten everything she wanted with the exception of affection or outward signs of love, was pulled into Bud's rage. Bud saw his opportunity of an easy life of the idle rich that he had been drawn to slipping away by what he considered Walter and Beulah's irrational intransigence. Louise lived with the gnawing fear of losing her handsome lover, the first and only one she had ever had.

Their sexual encounters continued unabated through the summer, usually at Bud's but frequently in motels, at Grandmother Jungquist' and on the ground on their frequent hiking trips in the hills north of Chatsworth. Bud's interest in Louise was primarily her wealth but his lust was genuine and he considered it frosting on the cake. The sex, however, provided only an interlude to what had become an obsessive hatred for Louise's parents. On one such trip on a Saturday in late August after the birthday party for Walter, they lay on a blanket in the afternoon shade of a tree, still only partially clothed; nibbling on sandwiches they had brought in a picnic basket. Bud was pensive and silent.

"What are you thinking about Pops?" Louise asked.

"What do you think I'm thinking about?" he answered sardonically.

"My parents, that's all we ever think about, anymore. They are spoiling everything for me, for us. I hate them"

"If it weren't for them, this could be our life. We could go to school at our own pace and study whatever we wanted," Bud stated wistfully, staring at the mountains to the north. Bud and Louise had become so immersed in their own selfishness and idyllic utopia that they began to assume a natural right to the comfort that the Overell wealth could provide. Bud had become, at times, sullen and uncommunicative because of his growing anger and frustration. It worried Louise. She was afraid that the beautiful life that she had found would slip away from her.

Bud started to finish dressing, shook his head and muttered, "Your f***ing parents!" Louise followed his lead and as she was finishing button her blouse, nearly shouted, "I wish they were dead! They've always hated me!"

They packed up their gear, walked the several miles to where the car was parked and started back to Flintridge. The sun had begun to set over the Pacific Ocean and they decided to stop at a drive-in and have hamburgers, fries and malts while they waited for the sun to set. On the way to the drive-in, Bud noticed a store along the road bearing the sign, The Trojan Powder Company. He made a U-turn and pulled into the small parking lot. The store was closed. There was a small sign advertising dynamite and other explosive material. Louise looked at him quizzically and he turned to her, stared at her briefly and drove on to the drive-in. This was the first time she realized that murdering her parents was on Bud's mind. She never said anything to him.

As they ate their hamburgers in silence, Bud was wondering what Louise was thinking, telling himself that he was not going to invest four years of his life, hoping that Walter and Beulah would change their minds about accepting him as a son-in-law, realizing that it most likely wouldn't happen. It appeared to him that they were approaching a crossroad. Louise knew he was thinking about the situation and realized that he was actually considering killing her parents. Oddly, she was not shocked. As they exited the drive-in, she nestled close to him put her left hand on the seatback behind him and fondled him with her right hand. Without saying a word, they both realized that their course of action, if it became necessary – still hoping it would not - was determined. All that was left was further attempts at changing the Overell's minds and, failing that, the planning.

Kathleen Heide, explaining why kids kill their parents outlines a number of scenarios.

They see no other choice. The youths killed a parent or parents in response to a perception of being trapped. In two of the five cases in which there was severe physical abuse, both were reacting to a perceived threat of imminent death or serious physical injury. In the three others, the children were experiencing terror and horror even though death and physical injury were not imminent. Interestingly, in these cases, the victims were defenseless: two were shot as they lay sleeping, the third as he sat watching television, his back to his son.

In the case of Bud and Louise, it was not physical abuse, it was the threat of denying something that they felt was vital to them and was rightfully theirs, the inheritance.

> **They are sorry for what they did**. *While many young felons brag about their acts, these youths seem uncomfortable with having killed. They knew their behavior was wrong, but experienced conflict over its effects—repugnance at the act they felt driven to carry out, yet relief that the victim could no longer hurt them or others dear to them. Their conflict seemed to result from a sense of their own victimization. They do not see themselves as murderers or criminals.[14]*

This comes very close to describing Bud and Louise.

The following week over the Labor Day weekend, Bud and Louise accompanied the Overells and Bud's grandparents, the George Rectors, on an 8-day visit to Catalina on the Mary E. Bud's sister, Pete, and his mother also went along. The boat was built to sleep 6 so they were crowded. Louise was reluctant to go because it meant there would be 8 days without sex. There just wouldn't be the opportunity on the small boat. Bud was a shameless sycophant. He insisted that he and Louise go, looking for an opportunity to ingratiate him with the Overells and telling Louise that it would give them an opportunity to continue to plead for their approval. He still had hope that as the Overell's saw him and Louise together, they would gradually accept the idea and accept the union. Being nearly devoid of any personality, Bud Gollum had no trouble in fawning over people, even people who displeased him.

When they lifted anchor at about 10:00 AM, Bud made it a point to show an interest in the boat and asked Walter for a complete tour availing him the opportunity to impress him but mostly to find the vital parts of the boat. His deadly plan had taken root in his mind.

---

14 Psychology Today, September 1, 1992

While Bud and his mother and sister were with Walter; with George Rector at the helm, Louise was able to engage her mother alone in the cabin.

"Mother, Pops and I want to get married," Louise began.

"What did you call him," her mother asked.

"I mean Bud and I want to get married."

"You call him Pops? Beulah insisted.

Actually, Louise was not sure why she used that nick name. She had just started using it and it stuck. Bud did not like it at first, saying, "I'm not your Pop, I'm not anything like him," but ignored it.

"Yes, that's a nickname that just came to mind and I like it, what's the difference? You are just trying to change the subject!" Louise replied with a little resentment in her tone.

"He is not your father; he is nothing like your father!" Beulah snapped.

Louise regained her composure. She was in control of her demeanor in nearly any kind of situation. Her face seldom displayed much emotion except when she was reacting to or with Bud. She had become completely mesmerized by him and totally committed to his world – whatever it was.

"I know he is not my father. He is my fiancé and I love him more than anyone in the world and I want approval of him from you and Father."

Beulah was strangely annoyed by her daughter's aplomb and expression of love for a young man she and her husband did not really like.

"You are both too young. You don't know what love is yet. By the time the two of you are out of school, your interests will have changed and you may not even like each other anymore," Beulah responded with a slightly condescending tone.

"That's what you and Father are counting on, hoping for, isn't it," Louise replied coolly.

Beulah was growing more impatient with the conversation and with her daughter's composure and determination and replied, "Yes."

"Mother, I will be eighteen on April 29 next year and will not need consent from you or Father. Get used to the idea, we are going to get married on that day," Louise responded with quiet emphasis.

Beulah totally lost her patience, if not her composure, and stated, "Well, you get used to this! You will NOT get our approval, and you can tell Bud he will not get our money! Your inheritance will be completely terminated! He will drop you like he did not even know you. Have you asked yourself why, when you have never had a date that suddenly this physically attractive young man seems completely enamored with you?"

Louise, still composed in her demeanor, was vitally hurt and seething underneath. "We can both get jobs and live in a trailer on the Stomel's property. We don't need your f***ing money."

Louise had never used profanity before and her mother was caught completely off guard. She slapped Louise. That had never happened before either. Louise's latent hatred for her parents jelled and she was prepared to do whatever Bud, her mentor as well as lover, required.

"Thank you, Mother," Louise replied as she walked out the door to look for Bud.

Unable to see Bud on deck, Louise retreated to the rear of the boat and stared at the wake of the clumsy slow moving Mary E. As she stood there, she was angry that her mother had slapped her but her real resentment was hearing her mother say what she already knew; she was ugly and would never be popular. Her mother had told her that the first really important thing in her life, her romance with Bud Gollum, was not based on love but on greed. She did not believe it but she admitted to herself that sometimes she worried about it. She knew that he enjoyed sex with her. His love making was passionate, spontaneous, and sometimes lecherous. She knew that he enjoyed it even more than she did. But when the sex was over, he often seemed withdrawn and almost non-communicative. Pete, his sister, told her that he was often that way with everyone. She always talked herself out of the doubt but it was always lurking in the back or her mind. Her trump thought was always, "I have the money...and I'm more than willing to share it with him if it makes us both happy." But now her parents were threatening to pull that away from her. She did not think they would do it. She had always gotten her way as long as it did not inconvenience them.

Shortly, her mother joined her at the railing and stood silently beside her for a while. Louise ignored her. Beulah put her hand on her shoulder and said, "Louise, I have never struck you before and I am sorry. I was just shocked at your language."

Louise was not moved by the apology and continued to stare at the wake, saying in her emotionless way, "It's not important, the slap was not what hurt..."

Beulah understood but did not know how to respond. She never had the ability, or the desire actually, to penetrate the dispassion that Louise had developed as armor over the years. As was her usual reaction, she withdrew her concern and without any commitment or sincerity replied, "We'll see, Louise, things have a way of working themselves out," and left her standing alone at the railing.

Louise, deeply withdrawn into her thoughts, never heard her or noticed she had left. She had retreated back into her early childhood. She remembered how differently her cousins were treated by their parents. Beulah's brothers' children were always being cuddled and held and played with by their parents. Even Louise's name sake, Grandmother Jungquist, was more affectionate with her other grandchildren. Louise would try to interact with her mother and father like her cousins did with their parents but was always awkwardly rebuffed. As she got older she quit trying. She found solace in the fact that she always had more toys than her cousins, had a bigger allowance and was always permitted to do anything she wanted. She was not closely supervised like they were. She learned to hold it over their heads, eventually alienating them too…to some extent…but she always maintained fairly good relationships with them, particularly Marjorie, her Uncle Fred's daughter.

She thought about the schools she had attended, always girl's schools. She was always the brightest one. She was also usually the least popular and always among the least attractive. She was never drawn into the cliques that little girls form. Her coping mechanism was a quick wit and a caustic tongue. The girls were afraid to be mean to her so they assiduously avoided her. She made herself not care. The studies were easy for her. She learned easily and always got the best grades. The ease of learning made school boring but she was never a discipline problem. Her teachers were never able to reach her but her grades were always good so they did not try.

She remembered how beautiful her mother was and how nice she looked in her clothes. Louise loved clothes and loved to shop. She always had plenty of money for shopping but she never knew how to dress. She often asked her mother to go shopping with her but she was always too busy; leaving the job to her governess. Her parents were both socially gregarious and she was never included like her cousins were with their parents. She spent more time with her governess than with her mother. She did not like her governess and the feeling was mutual. In fact, Louise did not like many people and the feeling was mutual. Her father was even less responsive than her mother. He always treated her kindly and was generous but Louise couldn't remember ever sitting on his lap or being hugged as her cousins were by their father. But she had a bigger allowance so she told herself it was OK.

Her parents entertained a lot. As she approached adolescence, she was sometimes allowed to hang around for a while (and be ignored by her parents' friends). Her father was not a handsome man. He was clearly overmatched and Louise assumed that she inherited her looks from her father. Drinking was always moderate at the parties and they often included her uncles and some of her cousins. As she approached puberty, she noticed that her mother received a lot of attention from the men. She also noticed that her mother enjoyed it. Her father was a hard worker and her mother often went to social events without him. He did not seem to mind. She sometimes went places in the evening with her friend from the Wilshire Church, Wilhelmina Rector, who had separated from her husband Fred.

There was always a lot of gossip within her parents' social groups. There was some hushed talk, talk that Louise picked up, of Beulah being promiscuous. There was even some talk of an earlier affair when Beulah was younger, before Louise was born, with a Senator who had been a pioneer in Flintridge. Her mother had kept a picture of him. He was some thirty years older than her mother so she discounted it…but she wanted to believe it. She felt that her father deserved it. She sometimes wondered if maybe Walter was not be her natural father. Sometimes she wanted to believe that too.

When Louise reached high school she attended a coeducational school. She continued to excel in her studies and skipped a grade. That was not a social problem because she was an early bloomer both intellectually and physically. Her breasts developed before most of her peers and, while always on the plump side, had a figure that attracted attention from the teenage boys, but she had bushy eyebrows (that her mother could have had groomed), an awkward chin, a poor complexion and dressed atrociously. He mother could have helped here also but never took any interest. Louise had a keen sexual interest in boys but was always so fearful of rejection that she always beat the young men to the punch and punished them with her sharp tongue and sometimes cruel humor. Most were intimidated by her and avoided her. Her aggressiveness, however, kept her out of harm's way as it related to typical teenage bullying or practical jokes. She remained a loner and told herself that was the way she wanted it.

She was starting classes next week at the University of Southern California and she looked forward to doing what she did best. She was going to major in Journalism and she would be spending the mid-weeks with Grandmother Jungquist in town and Bud would be attending Los Angeles City College just a few miles away. Between Bud's home, his grandparents' home and her room down the street, there would be plenty of opportunity for sex with Bud while they worked on overcoming Walter and Beulah's objection in whatever way it took! Louise was used to getting her way and she would this time as well.

Walter and Bud were in the engine room. Walter had been showing him around. Walter thought that Bud was buttering him up. He was right.

"Bud, what's really on your mind," Walter asked as kindly as he could.

Bud hesitated; looking down at his hands clasped in front and replied, "Walter…Mr. Overell… why don't you like me? You have known me and my family all my life and our two families are close. I just don't understand. I have always been respectful."

"It's Walter, Bud, you can call me Walter. I like you, Bud, that isn't the problem. Neither is it your ages, I just don't think you *or* Louise are ready to commit to each other. I don't think you really know each other well enough. You need to make some progress toward establishing yourself in the world. The same is true of Louise. Neither of you have any experience in a relationship. Both families, yours and Louise's, agree that time will prove your love or lack of it."

"*We* are sure of it."

"*We* are not."

Bud was in an inner rage but, as always, kept it under control.

"Louise will be eighteen in eight months. We will still be in love then. I will be in pre-med, working toward a career, and Louise will be studying at USC to be a journalist. You will have no reason to continue to oppose our marriage then unless you are permanently opposed to it for other reasons. We will get married then with or without approval from the families. I know my family will not object then." He immediately wished he had not gone so far but it was out.

Walter was openly annoyed. "I can't say what my feelings, or Beulah's will be then but if you marry her without our approval, you will be marrying a penniless woman," he said coolly and left Bud standing in the room.

Bud was angry with himself. He had not handled it well at all. He realized he had pushed too hard. Bud was a manipulator, or tried to be. He was never as clever or smooth as he thought he was but he had always been able to have his way with his mother. Like Louise's parents, Bud's father ignored him. He was somewhat of a mama's boy. His mother doted on him when she was around but did not spend nearly as much time with him or his older sister Wilafred as he would have liked. His mother and father did not get along and were divorced when he was just a boy. She was attractive and had an active social life. Oddly, she spent quite a bit of time with Louise's mother Beulah. She shortly remarried, marrying Joseph Stomel, a doctor, who had five children by his first wife, Ida, who had died in 1941.

Bud had never been close to his father, Fred. Fred Rector had been a relatively successful and busy stock broker. He also had two uncles, Lionel and Vivian, who remained in Chicago with the rest of the family. When his father and mother divorced, his only familial ties were to his mother's family, the George Rectors. His father, Fred Gollum was no longer in his children's lives. Bud tried to get close to his stepfather but Dr. Stomel, having his natural children to worry about, was never really interested. As is often the case in such marriages, he treated Bud and his sister with kindness but without warmth.

Bud was frustrated with life. He had not had a happy youth. His only social activity was in the Boy Scouts. He was large and strong but not athletic; he never took part in any organized sports. He was surrounded with wealth. His grandparents, the Rectors were wealthy, their close friends, the Overells were wealthy, Beulah Overell's family, the Jungquists was wealthy, most of the Overell's friends, as the Fred Davey family, were wealthy. Bud's family was upper middle class; his mother Wilhelmina's first husband was a stock broker and her second husband was a doctor. He grew up in a nice neighborhood. Most young men would be happy with that and use it as a starting place to launch a useful and successful life.

He joined the navy right out of high school. He probably did it out of patriotism; there was a lot of that going around in 1944. He loved boats and the sea. But it was more than patriotism that led Bud to enlist in the navy. Probably, the crowded household, which he was not used to, was also a reason. He was trying to postpone manhood and the responsibility of meeting the high standards of business and financial success in which he was surrounded. He had had some experience with menial jobs while he was in school and they bored him.

When Louise wrote him, he responded initially out of respect to the close friendship of the two families. But as they corresponded and met after his discharge, he began to see her as a means to achieving wealth and the ease and comfort of that life as he perceived it. He accepted the fact that she was physically unappealing. While he was a good looking young man, he had had no success with the opposite sex due to social awkwardness and a lack of self-confidence.

Beulah felt bad about her unpleasant confrontation with her daughter and retreated to the rear cabin, stopping by the galley to pull a coke out of the refrigerator and sat back to reflect. Minnie Rector, her best friend's mother and Bud's grandmother was there napping.

Beulah loved Minnie and her husband, George, after whom Bud was named. She did not feel guilt for not approving of their grandson but neither did she feel completely vindicated. The worst part was that she did not feel comfortable. How do you tell your best friend that you don't want her son as a son-in-law? As a matter of fact, she couldn't actually explain it – even to herself. She understood that Bud was after their money but in the social world of the wealthy, in some cases the idle rich, there was a lot of that. The free loaders, as it were, were often accepted and even welcome for any number of reasons. She saw something dark and foreboding in Bud. Walter was not so introspective in their discussion; he just did not like him.

She leaned back, took a drink from her coke and reflected on the last thirty years of her life. She had married Walter when she was twenty six years old in 1914. She had double dated with Bud's mother even after her and Walter had been married. After Wilhelmina had divorced Bud's father Fred, her and Walter had dated with her and her new boyfriend Joseph Stomel.

Beulah admitted to herself that she had never felt motherly to Louise and she felt guilty about it. She and Walter had been enjoying their active social life and her pregnancy interrupted it. She had been a very attractive woman and she enjoyed the attention and flirting. She had always been faithful to Walter but she got a strange satisfaction knowing that people thought she was promiscuous. She was aware of the rumors that she had an affair with Senator Flint years earlier. Senator Flint was a much older man and, while she was never attracted to him physically, was impressed with his position in the community and did nothing to discourage his fascination with her. Walter was unaware of the rumors or, having total trust in his wife, simply ignored them. Being in the real estate investment business was not hurt by having him as a friend.

Beulah and Walter had never wanted children. They were completely satisfied with their life together and the freedom of being childless. Beulah was thirty nine and Walter was forty four when the child who was destined to murder them was born. Obviously, she was not planned…or wanted. Beulah, more than Walter, resented the intrusion. She still had a good figure and still attracted attention from the men and Walter still felt good being with her in public. He was totally committed to her and loved her. Their life was good. In short, Louise was born without love.

Pregnancies take none months, normally. This one was no different. It was a long uncomfortable 9 months for the new mother. "Both unintended and unwanted childbearing can have negative health, social, and psychological consequences…..such childbearing has been linked with a variety of social problems, including divorce, poverty, child abuse, and juvenile delinquency….. As adults they were more likely to engage in criminal behavior, be on welfare, and receive psychiatric services. Another found that children who were unintended by their mothers had lower self-esteem than their intended peers twenty three years later."[15]

The unpleasant situation was exacerbated as Louise grew. She was not only unintended and unwanted; she was an unappealing baby and developed into an awkward and homely child – an ugly duckling without promise of morphing into a swan. Her mother would never have the vicarious pleasure of "showing" her daughter as other mothers in her family had. Louise had female cousins who were "cute" and "cuddly" and were the recipients of their parent's adoration and attention. Poor Louise was ignored by her parents and grandparents. Being unable to understand it, she would try to force attention which usually annoyed the adults and resulted in rejection and humility.

As she matured to puberty and adolescence, she adopted indifference as a defense mechanism and sought in other places for attention. Her parents were aware and ashamed of what they realized was neglect but were

15 http://www.prochoiceforum.org.uk/psy_ocr2.php

unable to modify their behavior and compensated by over indulging Louise in material things. She learned to use it as a tool. She compensated for lack of attention at home by studying hard and getting good grades. Louise was a very intelligent, albeit maladjusted, individual.

As a teenager, the normal sexuality developed, perhaps more than normal. This frustrated her even more. She was not only unattractive but socially unskilled. Even though she developed a buxom figure, earlier than her peers, she was ignored by the boys, many of whom felt intimidated by her biting wit.

Beulah saw this happening and felt bad about it. She saw her poor taste in clothing and despite appeals from her daughter to help her shop, could not bring herself to being involved and deferred to her governesses. She saw her heavy eyebrows and did nothing to improve her grooming. She saw Louise maturing physically and realized that there was a good figure lurking in her too heavy body but never encouraged diet or exercise.

Now, as Louise was about to become an adult and had a young man courting her, Beulah did not see the potential of a happy marriage and normal sex life for her. She saw, instead, a young man who wanted to exploit her wealth for personal gain. She had no proof of this but knew it instinctively. What she had to admit to herself was that her daughter was homely and not likely to attract the attention of a rather handsome young man. As time would prove, she was right in her instinct and right about Bud's dark insidious nature. If Louise was an intrusion into their social life, how much more inconvenient would it be to have another person living in their home. Bud was pushy. How soon would it be before he developed an assumption of proprietary rights? She shook her head and silently told herself that they could not let it happen.

As she was about to go back on deck, Minnie awoke, stretched and yawned and smiled at Beulah.

"I did not hear you come in; how long have I been sleeping?"

"I've been here for about 15 minutes and you were asleep when I sat down, so I'm not sure," Beulah replied. "Would you like me to get you a coke or a drink?" Beulah added.

"What time is it," she asked.

"It's 11:00 AM," Beulah replied

"Yes, please, a coke would be nice. Are you planning to have lunch on board or in Catalina?"

"I hadn't thought of it. We'll probably just snack on deck and have dinner on the island," she replied as she handed the coke to Minnie.

As Minnie sipped on her coke, she asked, "You look troubled, Beulah, what's on your mind? Are you and Louise quarreling again?"

"Still!"

"Still about Bud?" Minnie suggested

"Still about Bud, but it has escalated. I just now slapped her for her insolence. We have always given her everything and anything she wanted but this time we just can't do it."

Minnie took a sip on her coke, rolled the bottle around on her fingers, looked at Beulah and replied, "Well, dear, she will be eighteen soon and then it will be out of your hands."

"That is certainly true but Walter has told her – and Bud – that if they marry without our consent, she will be cut out of her inheritance."

Minnie took another sip and put the bottle down. "And what did they say when Walter told them?"

"They plan on going ahead. At least they say they are. Walter and I hope they are bluffing. Walter is not!"

Minnie understood the Overell's feeling that they probably viewed Bud as a "gold digger." She, herself, along with her husband, George, had discussed the possibility. She realized that was probably the prevailing and default opinion. Louise was an unattractive girl and Bud was not an unattractive young man; at least on the surface. She stared at the porthole and reflected…maybe everyone was being presumptuous in assuming that people had to be on a par in physical appearance in order to fall in love. She thought of the couples they had known who seemed to be on different playing fields in the "looks" department. She was also painfully aware of Bud's social awkwardness…but then she also considered his apparent inability to accept responsibility. It was always a problem since his father and mother had divorced years ago.

She looked back at Beulah, who she had known for thirty five years or more, and said in a consoling tone, "Things have a way of working themselves out. Maybe the two families can convince them to just go hold off until they are through school. It could be a test both of their commitment to each other and to making their own way in the world."

Beulah was relieved. Minnie was always so reasonable. She walked over to where Minnie was sitting, put her hands on her shoulders and said, "That is what we will do! I'm hungry; I'm going to stir up something for the crew to eat!"

She had several choices for sandwiches; she stepped out the door and called up to get the orders. She made sandwiches served with chips and cottage cheese and a small canned fruit salad. She told them there were cokes in the refrigerator. Walter had replaced George Rector at the helm so she took his plate up to him while the others ate in the tiny kitchen. She told him of her unpleasant conversation with Louise and he said his encounter with Bud hadn't gone much better.

Beulah asked, "Walter, what are we going to do?"

Walter replied, "We're going to enjoy the weekend. Things will work out. Don't worry about it."

Bud and Louise never had a chance to talk on board. There were too many people around but their eyes met as they ate their lunch and Bud shook his head almost imperceptibly to tell Louise it hadn't gone well. Louise rolled her eyes acknowledging that she understood. She really regretted going now. She and Bud needed to talk and it was impossible with so many people on the small boat.

In a couple of hours, while they were docking at Catalina, Louise found the opportunity to speak to Bud alone.

"Pops, why don't we make an excuse to eat alone when everyone goes ashore for dinner," Louise suggested.

"What about Pete, we couldn't just leave her with the old people, that would be rude," Bud replied.

"We could invite her along," Louise suggested.

"We couldn't do any serious planning."

"No but we could discuss my parents reactions and solicit her support. Don't you think?"

"Yeah, we can trust Pete," Bud agreed.

Later, as the group was getting ready to go ashore, Louise announced that she and Bud were going to get some takeout hamburgers and eat out on the beach. She invited Pete to go along with them. Pete was aware of what was going on and knew that the two of them needed to be alone and declined the offer.

"Are you sure, Pete?" Louise asked.

"Yeah, I'm really pretty hungry," Pete answered. It was actually true and she felt like a sit down meal.

Louise had brought a beach blanket and after they had eaten their hamburgers on a bench, they found a remote area where they were alone and could lie down to talk. They lay there for a few minutes on their sides facing each other and neither spoke. They embraced after a few minutes and fondled each other.

Louise asked, "Could we do it right here on the beach under the stars, Pops?"

Bud was aroused. The one true emotion he had for Louise was sex. He truly enjoyed that. It was better for him that with any other girl he had known but he pulled back and sat up. "No way, it's too risky, they have beach patrols and you are a minor. If a cop caught us, I would be in trouble!"

Louise sat up too and said, "I'll be so glad when I'm eighteen and we are married! I guess it did not go so well with my father today, huh?"

"I'm beginning to hate that condescending son of a bitch," Bud spit through clenched teeth. "I will be so glad when I no longer have to kiss his f****** ass!" Bud was becoming so obsessed with the Overell fortune that he was sometimes almost delusional. He began to consider the money, vicariously through Louise, as his and the Overells, particularly Walter, as evil roadblocks. "I assume it did not go any better with you mother."

"My mother slapped me," Louise said, "for the first time in my life she actually slapped me. I know she has wanted to many times but this was the first time."

"That bitch," Bud said quietly, "tell me about it."

"I used the F word. I have never used it in front of my parents before. In fact I hardly ever use it at all. I was just so frustrated. When she told me that Walter would cut me off if we married, I told her we did not need their f****** money."

This made Bud a little uneasy. Actually, they **did** need the money. That's what this was all about. The thought of taking a salaried 9-5 job, carrying a sack lunch and coming home tired every night to Louise was not the life he expected. He had to walk easy here and he had to make sure that Louise did nothing precipitously. Bud had the knack of hiding his anger and he would now too. He had to make sure that Louise was patient.

He toned down his demeanor and said, "Of course we don't **need** their money. We could get by but it's not just their money. It's also your money and if we are married, it will be **our** money and I don't want to be deprived of what is rightfully ours without a fight, do you?"

Louise understood what his message was completely. She felt very little love or even affection for her parents. She saw how her cousins' parents treated them; she was painfully aware that she got nothing from her parents except material things. She got along well with her cousins but she knew there was a twinge of envy for the things her parents gave her and she enjoyed it at the same time she felt even more envy for the attention her cousins received. She would have traded them in a second. She had an underlying fear that her relationship with Bud, her "Pops," was contingent on her inheritance. She would never let herself admit it to herself and hearing her parents insinuate it, or as her mother did earlier, say it, made her hate them.

"We have time, Pops; we'll make them come around. I know that if they knew you as well as I do, they would love you just as I do."

It was a boring eight days for Bud and Louise but they did find themselves alone on the boat several times long enough to satisfy their sexual needs. This shortened the trip for them. They returned just in time to start classes for the fall semester.

That September began the deadly game of cat and mouse. Walter and Beulah were in a sensitive situation. They just did not like Bud. In all likelihood, if they had liked Louise's suitor, the probability that he was a "gold digger" would have been overlooked. Bud was a son and grandson of long standing close friends. The Rectors, Bud's grandparents, were very close to the Overells and Jungquists. Walter consulted George Rector, who owned a yacht, when he purchased the Mary E. The three families attended the Wilshire Christian Church at Wilshire and Normandie. Beulah Jungquist Overell and Wilhelmina Rector double dated before and after they were married.

They were all good Christian people. The overells decided after considerable discussion that the best course of action would be to let the relationship wear out. They recognized Bud's social awkwardness and decided that, given enough exposure in social settings, Louise would come to see it too. They underestimated the degree to which Louise had fallen under Bud's spell. They also failed to recognize how much their neglect, their emotional abuse, of Louise had alienated her. Bud was physically attractive. Louise was not. He was also more mature. Bud not only had awakened her libido, he became a de facto surrogate father filling the void that her father's neglect had created. Her nickname for Bud, "Pops," was revealing. They included them in socials such as dances at the exclusive Annandale Country Club and to dinners with their socialite friends. It did not work. All it did was to whet Bud's appetite for what he saw as the life of the idle rich and Louise was too enthralled to notice anything clumsy about Bud.

Louise lived with Grandmother Jungquist during the week. She attended classes at the University of Southern California, Bud attended classes at Los Angeles City College, just a few miles north on Vermont. The Lundquist home and Bud's home were both close by. The situation was optimum for frequent contact. Bud would regularly pickup Louise at her grandmother's home and take her to school. On Fridays, he would pick her up from school, take her the Jungquist's where she would pick up her clothing and then drive her to Flintridge for the weekend. Bud's grandparents, George and Minnie Rector, lived a block away from Louise Jungquist. Bud and Louise were practically living together. There was ample opportunity for sex.

Bud's motivation in courting Louise was recognized by most everyone but Louise and she probably suspected it as well. The few classmates with whom Bud had any kind of relationship were aware. Philip Edward Mason, a classmate, asked him what the attraction was for Louise, whom he had met, and Bud replied, "Walter Overell is listed in the Southwest Blue Book."[16]

"What is the Southwest Blue Book," Mason asked.

Bud replied with a smile, "It only lists Millionaires."

---

16 The Southwest Blue Book is the Original Society Directory of Southern California with continuous annual publication since 1903. The late Lenora King Berry was appointed the responsibility of founding the first Society Directory list on the west coast. The Society Directory was named the Southwest Blue Book and has been published continuously by her family. Lenora published the book through 1950 when her brother, Warren W. King, became publisher. Gloria Berry Duthie, daughter of Lenora became Editor in 1951 and is assisted by her daughter, Deborah Duthie McKenna as Associate Editor.

Lester James Nelson, Jr., a longtime friend from the Boy Scout days, asked, "Then what's holding you back, what are you doing going to this school, or any school?"

Bud replied, "Her parents are against the marriage and have threatened to cut her off without a cent if she gets married. She won't be eighteen until the end of April and she can't get married without their approval until then anyway."

"Well, if they're going to disinherit her, what's the point in marrying her? She's not exactly a prize," Lester asked.

"That's over six months away. We will change their minds by then."

Both Nelson and Mason were called as witnesses for the prosecution and testified as to the conversations. Bud, of course, denied the conversation in his testimony.

Bud and Louise were together constantly. They talked to members of both families to solicit their support. They made it known that they intended to be married with or without the Overell's approval; with or without Louise's inheritance. Louise obtained a social security card and they went through the motions of looking for a trailer and talked to the Stomels and the Rectors about putting the trailer in the back of their property. But they both knew they were not going to live in a trailer and get jobs. Bud continued his solicitation of the Overells favor. Louise was an unwanted child. She wanted attention like her cousins got from their parents. Her behavior, sometimes bizarre, in seeking it annoyed the Overells. Now they were seeing it again in Bud's behavior; more subtle, more adult and better timed and planned but annoying just the same. Anyone who has supervised a worker with an abnormal desire to please understands this. Bud was always there to offer to go after things or do things for them. These are good traits and endearing when done spontaneously and sincerely; to the Overells, neither seemed to be the case with Bud.

The holiday festivities brought many opportunities for Bud to be with Louise's family. Bud bought and decorated the Christmas tree. While at the Flintridge home during the holiday, Bud overheard a conversation Walter was having on the phone. Walter noticed Bud standing in the kitchen within earshot. The conversation was from someone seeking a job on the Mary E. Walter at the close of the conversation remarked in the phone; "my future son-in-law will be helping me out on the Mary E." After he hung up, Walter told Bud that the call was from someone seeking employment on the boat and that he had told him that his son-in-law was going to be handling those chores. In his testimony, Bud used that conversation to prove that Louise's parents approved of the marriage. Realistically, particularly in view of the subsequent murders, it was Walter's way of putting Bud down; telling him that the only work or help he could expect as Louise's husband was in a menial job as a deckhand. He knew that this was not what Bud had in mind.

The holidays, Thanksgiving, Christmas, New Years with the parade and the Rose bowl game gave Bud and Louise many opportunities to be with her parents. Both Bud and Louise knew it was not working. Walter and Beulah also recognized that Louise was not going to break up with Bud. They all looked toward Louise's birthday on April 30, 1947 as the day of reckoning when everyone would have to show their hand. The Overells realized they had no control over Louise's decision after she was eighteen but were adamant in not allowing Bud into the umbrella of their affluence. He would have to get a job and support his family. They still did not expect that Bud would call their bluff and marry a penniless Louise.

After a round of sex at Bud's room when the Stomel's were gone, Bud brought the subject up.

"Louise, they are not going to approve, not ever. We have to eliminate them." Bud used a euphemistic term because he did not want to shock Louise.

Louise was not surprised or shocked but somewhat uncertain. She realized that had been the ultimate fallback option. "You mean, kill them, but how and when. What if we get caught?"

"Obviously, it has to be, or look like, an accident." Bud answered.

"Why couldn't we just go it without them?" she asked without conviction. She knew that she was not prepared mentally to assume a life of a 9-5 worker.

"Are you ready to get a part time job waiting on people in a diner living on what I can get through the GI bill for four years while we finish school?" Bud replied.

Louise, in reality, was not ready for that, but what bothered her the most was that Bud was telling her that without the money, there would be no marriage. She grew silent. Bud knew what she was thinking and looking out the window went on.

"Louise, you have a right for your share of that money. Don't let your parents continue to mistreat you!"

Louise felt little or no love for her parents. She realized that she had grown up in privilege and opulence but without a semblance of parental love. She would have traded the material abundance for their love; or thought she would. Bud had given her the only kind of love she knew. The fear of losing that was stronger than the repugnance of murder. She knew that Bud would actually do the act.

"How would you do it," she asked, "and when?

"I've been doing some thinking about it. I think it would be easiest to stage an accident that would kill both of them somehow on the boat. Let me think some more about it."

Louise cringed at the word "kill" and wished there were another softer work for it but realized that wouldn't change anything.

They continued their life going to school and seeing each other but things were different now. They now had a deadly resolve and the world looked differently to them. Bud had been thinking of explosives since the day that he and Louise had driven into the parking lot of the Trojan Powder Company in Chatsworth. He realized that there was no one with whom he could consult. He started reading about the different explosives and how they were used. He also realized that he would have to make sure that Louise was as involved as him to avoid the potential of her turning on him later out of remorse.

He decided that dynamite was the safest kind of explosive and easiest to buy. He studied articles on how to detonate it from a remote location and how to use it as a time bomb. He decided that the best and most believable accident he could stage would be an explosion on the Mary E while both Walter and Beulah and no one else were aboard. He read newspaper and magazine articles about accidents with explosives and he found that it did not always kill the victims. He learned that their location and activity at the time of the explosion was as important as the force of the blast. He finally concluded that the only safe way was to kill the Overells first and stage the explosion as a diversion and a logical cause of death.

There were always occasions when he and Louise were alone with the Overells on the Mary E. He would have to be prepared so he could act quickly. He told Louise of his tentative plan to wait for an opportunity when they were alone on the boat with her parents, kill them and set a bomb to explode after he and Louise had left. Louise wanted to know how he would kill them.

"How are you going to do it, Pops?"

"Do what?" Bud asked. He was not sure whether she was talking about blowing up the boat or killing the parents. "Blow up the boat or kill them?"

"Well, I really need to know about both," Louise replied as if she had thought of the complexity.

"Blowing up the boat will be easy; I will just have to learn a little more about explosives and how to detonate them. There is plenty of literature on that; explosives are used for many things. As for killing, it can't be a knife or a gun or any kind of poison. It will have to be done so that the injuries can be attributed to the explosion." Bud still hadn't worked out all the details of either the explosion or the murders. He was hesitant to say something like; "We will beat them to death" although he knew that was exactly what they would have to do. He knew also that he would have to convince her that she needed to help to prevent buyer's remorse down the road.

Louise brought it out. "You are saying that you are going to hit them in the head with something," aren't you. "That sounds so brutal."

"If it's done right and they die instantly, it will be painless. I will need you to divert their attention so they are surprised and it can be quicker and surer." This was the first time he had suggested her being involved in the actual murders. Louise did not reply. She hadn't thought about the possibility of actually being involved. She mused to herself that she was no more involved if she was in the room than if she was in the next room and let it happen.

She thought about the prospect of having to live in a trailer, of having to get a job. Even if she became a journalist, it would take four years and then menial jobs in the media. In those four years, or more, she would most likely have to work in demeaning jobs like serving tables or answering the phone. She thought of having to wait for Bud to finish medical school and all the hours doctors have to put in. Then she thought of an even worse, and although she couldn't admit it, more likely, scenario; Bud walking out on her. She thought of how he had changed her life from a homely virgin unloved by even her parents to having someone who loved her and showed her the carnal pleasure of unrestrained sex. Bud loved her. Her parents did not. She would miss Bud. She would miss the luxurious life she had known. The truth is, she would not miss her parents. It would not change her life at all!

They did not discuss it further that night. They had sex, he took her home and the next morning he picked her up at the Jungquist home on Manhattan and took her to school. The resumed their regular routine. They had taken one more gigantic step toward murder.

They continued the charade of preparing for marriage without her inheritance. They shopped for trailers and discussed it with Bud's family and his school mates. This went on through January and February of 1947. Louise's eighteenth birthday was looming large on the horizon. Something had to happen. Bud continued to read about explosives. He had decided on dynamite. It was safer and more controllable. Bud learned that a man was selling Trojan dynamite from his service station at the corner of Highland Avenue and City Creek Road in the San Bernardino area.

On March 2nd, Bud and Louise went to the service station which was owned and operated by Ben Smith who was a deputy on the San Bernardino Sheriff's Department and would testify against them later at their trial. They bought dynamite with detonators and told Smith they were using it to blow up a tree stump and asked for instructions. They were instructed to wrap the connection with tape if there was any possibility of moisture. Bud, along with Louise, took the dynamite to a remote area in the hills above Chatsworth where they had been a few times to picnic and make love. He practiced until he was sure of how to set it off with a timing device. It was not complicated and he learned quickly. He was ready and with this act, with Louise involved, he was sure that she was with him. Now they were ready, at the right time to make the larger purchase at the Trojan Powder Company.

Later he learned that Walter was going to spend the day of Saturday, the 15th of March on the Mary E having some work done and may have to move it into a boat repair spot. Beulah and Louise were going along to spend the day and evening on the boat. Bud took the opportunity to suggest that he might be of help rowing, moving the boat and bringing the mechanics out to the boat. Walter actually welcomed the offer and Bud agreed to meet them at the B Street wharf at 8:00 AM on the 15th.

When Bud picked Louise up from school on Thursday, he told her that they needed to talk and took her to a drive-in where they could talk in private. They ordered malts and Louise turned to Bud and asked, "What's up, Pop?" She was sure she knew what was going on.

"We're going to do it Saturday, after your father has the boat repaired," Bud told her.

"Why then," Louise asked

"When the mechanic is through, Walter will have to take him ashore and we'll be alone with your mother. We can take care of her while he is gone and then your father when he returns. Then we will rig up the explosion and go ashore. We will say that Walter sent us ashore for sandwiches."

"How are you going to do it, Pops?" Louise asked.

Bud turned to Louise, took her shoulders in his hands and said, "We, Louise, it's we. How are *we* going to do it? I have to know right now that you are with me on this. I'm doing it more for you than for me. If you have any doubts, let's drop it right now!" Louise was somewhat disconcerted by what she perceived as anger in Bud's reply. The repercussions of backing down flashed through her mind; losing Bud, returning to her lonely unfocused life, becoming an old maid without the sex that Bud had shown her.

Bud was a psychopath. He felt no remorse and he would feel no guilt. He had seen death when in the war in the navy. The sight of bleeding and mutilated bodies would not bother him. He had nothing but resentment for the Overells. They had treated him with disdain…as if he were a servant. He had humiliated himself in trying to win their approval; approval that never came. He could contemplate or plan killing someone with the same emotional detachment as he would have if he were planning a picnic with Louise. Louise, on the other hand, while emotionally disturbed by her lack of love, was vulnerable to guilt and it was difficult for her to anticipate the actual act. The whole thing seemed surreal to her. It was like a dream in which she had no control over the unfolding events. In the back of her mind, she felt that this dream could not have a good ending but she was in Bud's spell; it was either Bud or her parents. She loved Bud, or thought she did. She had no feelings for her parents other than dependence and what Bud was planning would remove the dependence.

"I'm in all the way, Pops, I know it has to be done if we are to be happy," Louise said as she looked at him and put her hand on top of his on her shoulder. "How are *we* going to do it?"

"With a ball peen hammer; there's one that's kept in the engine room. I know it sounds brutal but it will be over instantly. You can engage her in conversation and I will bring the hammer out of the engine room and walk in behind her. It will be over in a second. She won't feel a thing." Louise shuddered but nodded her head in assent.

"When your father returns, when he is walking down the steps to the cabin, I'll hit him from behind and it will be all over. Then, I'll row ashore, pick up the dynamite and rig the explosion."

"Oh pops! Please don't leave me alone on the boat with the two dead bodies," Louise pleaded.

"It won't take me 20 minutes," Bud said softly in a conciliatory tone.

"Then, take me with you," she insisted.

"That will slow us up and attract more attention," Bud argued. Louise sipped on her malt as she thought of alternatives. It came clear to her and putting down her malt, she turned to Bud.

"Pops, you have to have the dynamite already aboard. What if something happens after we have killed my parents and you can't get the dynamite? We'll be stuck with two dead bodies with no explanation." Bud reflected a while on this. It made sense. He thought about the possibility of someone finding the dynamite. How would that be explained? While it wouldn't be a natural or even logical assumption that he or Louise was involved, it would put such a crimp in the plan that it would have to be put off indefinitely. He stared out the window as he reflected on the problem. Louise became nervous with his silence. She was sure she knew what he was thinking.

"How big is the box that the explosives are in?" she asked.

"Not big, about the size of a small grocery box." He answered, not sure where she was going.

Louise went on, "I know a spot in the cabin where I sleep where it would never be seen. It's a storage closet that no one ever opens unless they want to store something. Even if someone opened it to put something in it, the box wouldn't be noticed." Bud knew of the closet and agreed that it was perfect.

"I know the closet," Bud exclaimed. "You're right, it is ideal and it would be much better to already have the stuff on board. I can come early Saturday and bring it aboard before anyone gets here. I can rent a skiff. We'll need one anyway." Louise was relieved that she wouldn't have to remain on the boat with her dead parents. She was not sure she could do that.

"When are you going to buy the dynamite? Are you going back to the place in San Bernardino?" Louise asked. She hadn't felt comfortable with the guy at the service station.

"We can buy it Friday after I pick you up from school. We'll buy it from that store we stopped at a few months back when we had been picnicking out by Chatsworth. I've checked them out. It's called the Trojan Powder Company and they keep it in stock. If we bought it at the same place it would attract more attention."

On Friday, March 14th, Bud picked Louise up at school and they drove to the Trojan Powder Company in Chatsworth. They bought 50 pounds of 7/8 inch 40% dynamite and 50, No. 6, 4-foot caps according to the sales receipt later found in a camera in Bud's possession.[17] The total bill came to $16.04. The salesman was L. A. Hill who, when later called to identify them, would be unable to say they were, or were not, the couple who bought the dynamite. The customer's name, as signed by Bud, was R. L. Standish, 208 West Blvd., in Palmdale. Bud also signed the name Robert Comstock for whom he had told Hill he was buying the dynamite, saying it was to be used for mining.

After buying the explosives, Bud drove Louise to her grandmother's home on Manhattan where she picked up her clothes and drove to the Overell's home in Flintridge. After having dinner with them, Bud drove home. The next morning, he arose at 5:00 AM and drove to Balboa. He parked his car on Central Avenue[18] at A St. He rented a skiff, rowed out to the Mary E and stowed the box in the location that Louise had suggested. He then went back ashore to await the arrival of Louise and the Overells.

The Overells arrived first, shortly after 8:00 AM and parked near Bud. A short time later, Bud saw Louise drive onto A Street from Bay Avenue. He motioned to her and she parked behind him. All three cars were close together. When they got to the corner of A St. and Central, they met Walter and he told them to hurry down to the dock. Mrs. Overell was already in the rented skiff with the mechanic. Bud, Walter and Louise joined them. Bud rowed the five of them to the Mary E where they all boarded. As they headed for the boat where they would murder her parents, Louise reflected on what was happening. She fantasized in grizzly satire if she should kiss them good-bye. She thought back of the time when she was a small child when she tried to climb on her mother's lap like her cousins did on their mother's laps and was rebuked by her mother, pushing her away saying, Louise, you'll wrinkle

---

17 Dynamite comes in various strengths and sizes. Usually, an 8 inch stick, 1 ¼ inch in diameter weighs a half pound. This sale must have included at least 100 sticks.

18 Central Avenue, since 1947 has been changed to Balboa Blvd so references to Central Avenue in the narrative would refer to Balboa Blvd. on the maps.

my dress. There were many such rebuffs by both parents at the same time her cousins, the Jungquist children were loved by their parents.

When they were all on board, the mechanic, Ted Junkemeier, and Walter went to the engine room while Bud and Louise stayed on deck studying Spanish. Beulah went to the forward cabin. The mechanic worked on the boat most of the day. He and Walter were on and off the boat several times and at one time drove to Santa Ana looking for a part. At one point the Mary E was taken to Virge's Landing, a boat repair dock, and serviced there. It was returned to its original spot in the harbor in the afternoon and the mechanic worked on it well into the evening.

Bud and Louise left the Mary E twice during the day; the first time they went to a hardware store. In his testimony, he said it was to get boat repair hardware but it is doubtful that he would do that without Walter's direction and there is no mention of that in his testimony. It is more likely that he picked up something for arming the explosion. The second time, still in the morning, they had a hamburger and a malted milk. It was around 9:00 PM when Walter Overell left the boat for the last time to take Ted Junkemeier, the mechanic, to his car. That's approximately 13 hours after Louise first arrived at the boat. It's hard to understand how a normal person could function normally for that long, being close to her mother most of the time, knowing that at the end of the day she was going to help murder her parents. The incredulity of the situation may well be why the jurors found it difficult to believe it…despite the incredible stretch of logic it took to believe otherwise.

With Walter off the boat, it was time to put their plan in action. Beulah was reading in the forward cabin next to the engine room warming herself with a lap robe. Beulah's chair faced away from the door. Bud went into the engine room and brought the hammer with him and stood outside the door waiting for Louise to distract her mother with conversation. Louise realized he was there and pulled a chair up in front of her mother. Beulah was not ready for another confrontation. "What is it this time Louise?" she asked, impatiently. Her mother's attitude made it easier for Louise. She noticed Bud approach her mother from the rear and her eye glanced up at him; this caused Beulah to turn to her right just as Bud raised the hammer. She screamed "BUD" and threw up her hand in front of her face absorbing most of the force of the hammer. The first blow broke her fingers and made a gaping wound in the temple area just above the left eye. It did not kill her and she continued to scream as she turned to Louise. Bud quickly struck her several times in the back of the head and her screaming stopped. Her eyes still open, Louise could see her eyes gloss over in death and she became hysterical. She was angry with Bud because he told her it would be painless.

Bud was alarmed. He could see the plan falling apart. He went to Beulah's body and pulled her eyelids shut as her head slumped forward. He calmed Louise down and told her it was her fault for looking past Beulah and drawing her attention to him. Louise knew that she had done that. There was not as much blood as he had feared. He had a few splatters as well as did Louise. He decided that it would go much smoother with Walter if he did it alone. He put his arm around Louise and told her that there was absolutely no turning back now and she nodded.

"Louise, I think it would be better if I handled your father alone. You can stay back here with your mother." Bud suggested.

Louise had calmed down. "I don't want to stay here. I'll go on deck and wait for Father while you are preparing the explosives. When I see him, I'll call you and then I'll go into the engine room and wait for it all to be over."

It sounded like a good idea, and he agreed. "Let's get started then." It was about 10:00 PM and he was nearly finished when Louise called to him. They changed places and he went to the railing where Walter was climbing up the ladder to come aboard. Bud followed him as he crossed the deck and started down the stairs to the forward cabin and engine room and hit him in the head with the hammer. Walter never saw it coming and it was all over. He fell down the stairs to the floor of the engine room which was next to the forward cabin. To make sure he was dead Bud jabbed him in the back of the head with a pipe lying nearby. In the unlikely event of an autopsy, the different kind of wounds would make it appear more likely that shrapnel had caused death.

Bud put the bulk of the dynamite in the forward cabin with the timer and about thirty remaining sticks in the engine room. He washed the hammer in the bath room and dropped it on the floor. He assumed the main blast would detonate the remainder of the explosives. He poured gasoline in the forward cabin and the engine room assuming the explosion would start a fire which would finish obliterating the evidence. Bud did not realize that dynamite was used to extinguish fires on oil wells by using up all the oxygen.

Bud changed his blood stained tennis shoes and his shirt, leaving them in the engine room assuming the fire would destroy them. Louise changed clothes but wrapped hers in the blood stained lap robe they removed from Beulah. It was about 11:00 PM. Bud set the detonator to go off at 11:45 PM, took Beulah's keys from her purse and they rowed ashore. Louise had completely overcome her hysteria now and was feeling anxious for it to be over so they could start their life of leisure and luxury together. They went directly to Bud's car parked on Central Avenue between A St. and B St., left the dirty clothes in Buds turtle back, and walked to the Casino Café on A Street near Bay Ave.

They ordered hamburgers and cokes. Bud only ate half of his and Louise ate hers and the rest of Buds. Louise asked him why he was not hungry.

"Are you worried about the dynamite going off, Bud?"

"No, it will go off. It worked before and it will work this time." He replied casually, hiding his anxiety. "If it doesn't, we'll go back aboard and fix the problem. We have time."

They paid for the food and left the café just as the explosion rocked the Harbor at 11:45 PM. They felt elated but realized that they would soon be under scrutiny and would have to display normal reactions to the death of the Overells. Holding hands, they began running up A Street toward Central Avenue so they could reach the skiff at the B Street landing. When they reached the B Street landing there was a crowd and Louise went into her near hysteria act going from person to person asking if their parents got off and screaming for someone to go rescue them. Not being exactly sure of what they should do or how people would expect them to react, they retreated back to where her parent's car was parked on Central Avenue near B Street. Louise got in the car and Bud talked to Newport Beach Police Department Officer Lawrence Goddard. It had been Goddard and his partner George Calihan who saw the explosion, saw the boat sinking and called the fire department.

Bud approached Officer Goddard and said, "That is the Mary E. My fiancée's parents were aboard. What should we do? Can we row out there and see if they're OK?"

Officer Goddard was not so sure but he did not know any details at all so he said, "I guess it would be OK, where is your fiancé?"

"She's in her parents car right over there," pointing to the car. "She is half crazy with worry."

"OK, but when you get out there, check with any officials there before you go aboard," Officer Goddard advised.

Bud agreed over his shoulder as he went to the car and to get Louise. "We have permission to row out the Mary E," Bud told her! "Hurry!"

They half ran and half walked to the rented skiff and rowed out the short distance to the boat. The Coast Guard officials were already there and told them they couldn't board. Bud told them that Louise's parents were on the boat and asked if they were OK. The officer hesitated and told Bud that there were two bodies on board and that he should take Louise ashore. He rowed back to the B Street landing and walked toward the Overell car. He met Officers Goddard and Calihan there and they confirmed that the blast was a double fatality. He asked if he could take Louise home because she was near a break down. The Officers, without seeing any identification, released Bud to take Louise from the scene.

Bud decided it was best to take Louise home in his car because it had so much evidence in it. He left the Overell car and Louise's parked on Central Avenue. He drove back to Los Angeles and stopped at his parents' home and while Louise waited in the car told them what had happened. Neither of the Stomels came to the car to offer condolences according to Bud's testimony. He also testified that he called Louise Jungquist's home and asked the maid to tell Louise's Uncle Fred to arrange a chaperone for the Flintridge home. There was no corroboration of that call and he did not state or was not asked under cross examination why he did not speak to someone else at the Jungquist home to inform them of the tragedy. It was only a few hours after the explosion and he had no way of knowing if they had been told.

Actually, Bud and Louise, now murderers, wanted to be alone to breathe a sigh of relief over what they thought was a successful family coup d'état. They were both emotionally drained and physically tired but when they reached Flintridge, they spent a half hour ransacking the house to see what they had won. Louise had the lingering image of hearing the bones in her mother's fingers and her skull breaking, or being crushed, and had to fight the unwelcome sense of guilt but her overriding emotion was that she was now in charge of the family estate; it was hers and she did not have to ask her parents ever again for anything. After going through the house, they went to Louise's room and erased the gruesome images with unrestrained sex. Louise went to sleep thinking that this was going to be their new life.

The maid, Mary Pritchett, would tell the police after the arrest how she found the house when she got there early Monday morning. "They had completely ransacked the house, opening all the drawers in every room, throwing things on the floor and scattering papers, boxes and clothing about the rooms." She would also tell investigators that Mrs. Overell never gave her keys to anyone and that after she went up to her room she heard Bud and Louise "laughing heartily" and having a good time downstairs.

They arose early on Sunday because they assumed that family members would be visiting. They had breakfast and Yvonne, Fred Jungquist's daughter, and her husband Fred Davey came over. Bud and Louise were playing ping pong. Fred Davey was surprised if not shocked and said to Bud that he really needed to take a look at his behavior because it might not look right to some people. There was no indication at this time that murder was suspected and Fred was thinking more of how it would seem to the Jungquists to see their sister's daughter and her future husband taking her death so lightly. In fact, it offended Fred and he was only extended family through marriage to Yvonne. He had been aware of the family's aversion to the marriage of Louise and Bud and he really hadn't approved himself, though he realized that it was none of his business.

Yvonne's father, Fred Jungquist, also came over and talked to the young couple...mostly to Bud. Fred, like his son-in-law, never had warmed up to Bud. He was going along with Beulah's decision to hold it off and hope that it would run its course. Fred may have been the first to have suspicion.

He asked Bud, "Where in the hell were you and Louise when it happened. I thought the four of you were together."

"Mr. Overell asked us to go ashore and buy some sandwiches and milk," Bud replied. He knew that Fred did not like him and the feeling was mutual but he had the disadvantage of not being able, under the code of the toady, to express his true feelings – even in voice inflection. Fred recognized his insincerity.

"That doesn't make any G** D***** sense. If you were all going home, why did not you just stop and eat ashore?" Fred asked incredulously. Bud was annoyed at his tone but in view of the fact that he had just killed his sister and others might be asking the same question, replied carefully and under control.

"Well, Mr. Jungquist, you know Mr. Overell and that I'm trying to win his favor. I pretty much do what he asks me without question. He told me that he wanted to air the boat out because of the strong odor of gasoline."

Fred persisted. "Why did it smell of gasoline, working on an engine doesn't develop gasoline fumes; and why couldn't he just leave the windows open all night?" Bud had no response and was silent. Fred was still shaking his head in confusion, grieving about his sister when they were interrupted by Fred Davey, Yvonne, and Louise, who had gone after take-out food. Fred was surprised at Louise's apparent lack of mourning or display of grief. He thought that maybe she was still in shock and the gravity of the situation hadn't hit her. He and the Jungquists were grief stricken over Beulah and Walter's death and it bothered him that Louise was laughing and playing ping pong and seemingly unaffected. He blamed Bud. He reflected on the tragic irony of the situation. His sister and her husband had been so adverse to having Bud as a son-in-law and sponging off them that they would disinherit their only child to prevent it. Now, it appeared that Bud, through his control of Louise, was going to inherit everything Walter had worked so hard for. What a reason for staging an "accidental death" was a fleeting thought but he shamefully dismissed it – not because of Bud but because of his niece.

Before he left, he made it a point to talk to Louise and Yvonne while Bud was out of the room. He felt strongly that Bud was controlling her and he did not trust him. He told Louise that she should get away for a week or two with Yvonne or Emmanuel's daughter Marjorie. He knew that Louise looked up to them. They were a few years older than her. Yvonne expressed an interest and Louise courteously said she would think about it. He left after the conversation and did not see Louise again until the next day.

Fred and Yvonne spent the rest of the day at the Flintridge home and acted as chaperone that night. In 1947, appearances were more important than today. Although the family knew that Bud and Louise were intimate on an ongoing basis, protocol demanded that they not spend the night together alone. The Jungquists and Overells both had strong Christian beliefs although they did not regularly attend. Fred had an even stronger aversion to Bud than Fred Jungquist. He was not close to the Jungquists but respectful. Fred and Yvonne's mother had divorced and Ida, for whom Yvonne was named, had remarried. He was closer to Ida and her new husband than with Fred Jungquist. Earlier, when the question of the status of Bud and Louise's relationship was before the family, he had a conversation with Bud when they were alone. Bud remarked that he and Louise might elope. Fred had suggested that this wouldn't be fair to Walter and Beulah and discouraged it. He had asked Bud how he would support Louise and Bud replied that he hadn't thought about it. In his testimony at his trial on cross examination, he stated that the conversation about eloping had been entirely facetious and denied the remark about supporting Louise. Fred Davey had testified earlier for the prosecution.

Later in the afternoon, between ping pong games, Fred saw Bud and Louise running around back of the house arm and arm and laughing. Later he commented again about Bud and Louise's cavalier attitude one day after Walter and Beulah had been killed. Bud shrugged it off and remarked that he had seen a lot of death when he was in the war. Fred thought this was an inappropriate response and replied that seeing someone killed in the war did not equate to the death of close friends or family and said that he personally felt a deep sense of loss because of the death of the Overells. Bud did not respond but later would deny the conversation.

Bud had a bad bruise on his forearm and Fred asked him how he got it. Bud replied that he got it while working on the engine on the Mary E. Fred also asked him about a bent ring he was wearing and Bud told him he bent it rowing the boat the day before. Later he would deny the time and substance of the conversation.

Later in the evening, Bud's sister Pete and her fiancé came by and Louise asked her if she would move in the Flintridge house until her and Bud were married and she agreed. Marjorie, Emmanuel Jungquist's daughter, came over and spent the night. Saturday night, Bud and Louise had no chaperone and Sunday night they had three. This was no doubt a reflection on the family's concern for appearance and they wanted to make sure it did not happen again. Fred Davey thought the evening was bizarre. Bud was his usual vapid self – that seemed to never change – but Fred thought Louise acted more like they were Christmas visitors. Later, when he heard of the arrests, it all came together for him.

Louise was actually having a hard time with the visits. She would rather be alone with Bud who could offer assurance to her and keep things in perspective. She was totally under Bud's spell. She had just collaborated in the murder of her parents. She knew she wouldn't miss them - they had never really been parents anyway – but she knew murder was wrong and she had fleeting thoughts of the sound of her mother's fingers and skull cracking from the hammer blows and the of the blood oozing onto the floor from her fathers crushed skull. She needed Bud to keep her focused on the good times that lie ahead and how her parents were mistreating her by denying her inheritance.

Louise asked her neighbor, Mrs. Herbert Van Zwoll to spend Monday night with them as a chaperone. Mrs. Van Zwoll later told investigators that she saw Bud open the safe and hand some papers to Louise and gave Louise Mrs. Overells expensive mink coat which she wore to the Overell's funeral after she was under arrest.

Bud's sister, Pete, came over and they moved some clothes out of one of the bedrooms to make room in the closet for her. They told Mrs. Van Zwoll that Pete was going to stay in the Flintridge home for a while. Tuesday night, Mary Pritchett stayed in the house with Bud, Louise and Pete.

Tuesday morning, Bud got up early and took his sister to school at 7:00 AM and then he and Louise went to the office of a Mr. Neice, an Attorney, and met Louise's Uncle Emmanuel there. Emmanuel had made the appointment. Mr. Neice showed them the Overell will. From there, Neice, Emmanuel, Bud and Louise went to the Farmers and Merchant's bank. This was the bank that was handling the Overell estate. They met officers of the bank there and they discussed financial arrangements she would need while they were settling the estate. She told them she wanted to continue living in the Flintridge home.

Bud and Louise would spend just one more night in the Flintridge mansion. The next day they were arrested for the murder of her parents.

Part V

REQUIEM FOR BAD SEED –
THE FATE OF BUD AND LOUISE

On February 25, 2009, George Rector Gollum, known by family and friends as Bud, died in ignominy in Wasilla, Alaska. The hypothetical question, "If a tree falls in the forest and no one hears it, does it make a sound," is often asked in a discussion of reality. When Bud Gollum died in Wasilla, no one knew it and it did not make a sound – or a difference. His death didn't even rate an obituary or item in the local newspaper. It is probable that his two children living in a different state or his two ex-wives, if still alive, were unaware of it; and if they did know of it, or when they learned of it, there probably was not much grieving.

On August 24, 1965, 3400 miles away in Las Vegas, Nevada, his partner in crime died of alcoholism while contemplating suicide.

Eighteen years earlier, on October 5, 1947, when Bud and Louise were acquitted of murdering her parents, they were the toast of the public. The young couple was free to live a romantic life of luxury with Louise's inheritance. But when the verdict was read, they left the court in different cars. The trial and bickering between the attorneys and between Bud and Louise's families had created an irreparable rift. They were both headed for disaster but on different routes.

Louise found out that the estate was not as much as she had thought. Accounts of what she inherited vary but they all agree that it was a fraction of what she and Bud expected. Being under age at the time of the death of her parents, she was assigned co-guardians, her mother's two brothers, Emmanuel and Fred Jungquist, who set up a trust from which she just drew the interest with the principal becoming available at age 21. The consensus put the amount of the interest on the insurance policies and the estate at approximately $800 per month with the principal of $310,000 becoming available when she reached age 21. Both the boat and home on Los Robles were sold.

The murder and trial strained the unity of her family. Her uncles Emmanuel and Fred testified against her and believed she was guilty. Her Uncle Fred and Cousin Marjorie supported her; but most likely with considerable doubt. Her grandmother, Louise, matriarch of the Jungquist family, distanced herself from Louise. Louise and her cousin Marjorie planned a trip to Europe but Louise had an emotional breakdown in the San Francisco Bay Area and was hospitalized in a sanitarium for several weeks. Uncle Fred and Marjorie were by her side.

At the very best, her relationship with her family was strained – even with those like Uncle Fred and Marjorie who expressed support. The question and doubt was always there but never brought up in conversation. Those who did not support her avoided her. They were in the majority. The media continued to write or speak of her as someone who had beaten the system and had "gotten away with murder." The public, the ones who had followed the trial and had celebrated her acquittal, when the emotion evaporated, began to believe so too.

She began to drink. She had never been a drinker but the constant nightmare of watching Bud murder her mother and father drove her to it. The immediate afterglow that Bud pulled her into, thinking that the two of them would live the rest of their lives at 607 Los Robles Drive wallowing in the luxury of her father's success soon evaporated. Ironically, neither Bud nor Louise realized that Walter was not a member of the idle rich and that his wealth was not static but dynamic and was based on his ability to earn in the future not merely on what he had earned in the past.

She was lonely. She had enrolled in school at UCLA for the spring semester and was waiting for classes to start. She thought she could force the horror of that night from her mind with what she had excelled at earlier – studying. She was living on an allowance from her inheritance which was not enough to afford tuition at a private school like USC and none of the Jungquists were willing to pay it for her. Louise was, for the first time, on her own. She was not sure how she would be able to handle a public school. She had never attended one. She had no idea what kind of people attended public schools.

In late January, she ran her car into another car at an intersection. She had been drinking so she didn't stop. The woman she ran into got her license number and she was later arrested on a hit and run warrant. She appeared in court and was fined. She had no social life. She had no friends to turn to. Her cousins were polite but the relationship lacked warmth. The suspicion and distrust grew. She decided to move into an apartment. She didn't have to overcome a lot of resistance. She hadn't seen Bud or any of the Rectors or Stomels, since the trial was over. She knew Bud was still in town. She dreaded the possibility of running into him. She had heard that Bud's stepfather refused to let him live with them.

In August, 1948, while attending a party she met a Los Angeles policeman named Robert Johnston[19] who recognized her from her pictures in the papers and struck up a conversation.

"Hi Louise, I'm Robert Johnston. I'm on the LAPD and I recognized you from the big trial down in Orange County a couple years ago. How are you doing?"

Louise was uncharacteristically rattled. This was the first time a stranger had approached her on the subject. "I'm OK," she replied with a little sarcasm, "I'm looking forward to the day that strangers will no longer recognize me."

"Does it happen a lot?" Robert asked.

She loosened up a little and replied, "Not really, in fact you're the first one who has recognized me...at least the first one who has admitted it. Maybe people are afraid I will go berserk and hit them in the head with a hammer!"

"Am I in danger, Louise?" Robert joked.

"What do you think? Are you nervous?"

"I'm quivering in my boots," he joked. "Can I get you a drink?"

"Smirnoff and tonic," she replied. Since the trial she had replaced malted milks with vodka.

Louise stared at him as he walked toward the bar. She sized him up. He was smaller than Bud but better looking. He had blond hair and blue eyes.

---

19 Not his real name, he is still living.

His nose was just a little too large and he had large eyes and a high fore-head. Louise was still painfully aware that she was not attractive but she had learned to dress to accent the better features of her figure. She had a low cut blouse on which exposed a generous amount of cleavage. She didn't really like to dress this way but all the fashion magazines promoted it and it was how the movie stars dressed.

He returned shortly with the drinks and they found a place to sit down. They sat in silence for a few minutes and took a few sips of their drinks. He was drinking beer.

"So what are you doing now? Going to school, working, playing profes-sional tennis or doing the shuffle board tour?" Robert joked.

"I attended UCLA last semester but I'm not on the tennis team, and I'm too young to hit the bars but I manage to find something to keep from get-ting too dry. Is that where you drink, in the cowboy bars? You don't look the type."

"I'm a cop, remember? I can't afford to drink in the piano bars. It's shuffle board and pool and cheap beer or good foreign beer at home. You need to let me show you the other side sometime. You might like it…but after you hit 21"

"You're not married then?" Louise asked.

"I'm divorced."

"Then OK," Louise said.

"OK, what?"

"You can show me the other side sometime," Louise said putting her drink down. She was starting to stir inside. Robert was good looking and fun. She hadn't been with a man since she and Bud had been arrested on March 19, 1947. That was 15 months ago. The last man she had sex with murdered her father and mother with her approval… and as she watched. Somehow she associated the sex act with the murders. She was guilt ridden and tormented every waking hour. She was not doing well in school and was not really inter-ested. She couldn't concentrate. The only escape she had from thinking of seeing Bud crush her mother's skull with a hammer was drinking herself to sleep. It's true that she hadn't loved her mother or father and that they had never given her the warmth that she saw her cousins receive but that was not why she agreed to help Bud kill them. She did it because he was the first person who had shown her any love; carnal and perverted, but love. The only kind of love she had known. She also came to realize during their vicarious bickering through the attorneys and the two families during the trial that he was only interested in the wealth. Now, she was not sure she could have a normal relationship with a man – sexual or otherwise. It was time to find out.

Robert asked her to have dinner with him the following Friday and she agreed. He was to pick her up at her apartment at 7:00 PM. They spent the rest of the evening together at the party having a few dances and a few drinks. They left early and he walked her to her car and kissed her goodnight. It was an entirely appropriate kiss that lingered a little longer than she expected. She didn't mind and began looking forward to Friday. Maybe she could shake the guilt and find some peace.

Robert was recently divorced and waiting for it to be final. His first wife was a beautiful woman involved in the movie business. She was a cheater. He didn't want that again so he was thinking that a woman who had some sex appeal without attracting a lot of attention from others might be a pleasant change. The fact that he knew, or thought, that she had inherited a fortune didn't diminish her appeal.

Robert picked her up exactly at 7:00 PM as he had told her. Cops not only like being on time, they get in the habit, at least most of them, of being precise. Cops didn't make much in 1949 but most of them spent more than they could afford on their vehicle. Robert was no exception. He drove a 1949 Mercury Coupe with integrated skirts, white walls and every option available. It had set him back $2900 – a lot of money in 1949! When he opened the door to let Louise in, he was glad that he had splurged. He was opening the door for a millionaire, or so he thought. But her money was not on his mind. At this point, marriage was the last thing on his list of things to do. He was just getting out of one and liked the single life. His interest in Louise was sex – the same as most young men letting their date into their car in Los Angeles that night. Robert had followed the trial like most everyone. He remembered the letters reproduced in the Los Angeles Examiner. Like most everyone else, he thought she was probably guilty but, again like everyone else, thought she was manipulated by Gollum and was actually another one of his victims. And he had a slight case of celebrityitis. He was looking forward to having an affair with a famous person – even though in this case, it was more of an infamous person.

As she entered the car, Louise reflected on the last time a young man had opened a car door for her. It was March 19, 1947, the day she and Bud were arrested. She was not as sure as her date that she was going to have sex that night. She wanted to but was not sure she would be able to. She was not sure it wouldn't activate the demons, or more aptly, energize them; they never left her until the vodka numbed her and gave her temporary respite. To her, the sex, if it happened, would be therapy. Louise had lost a lot of weight due to her replacement of food with alcohol. Her figure was better than it was in 1947…but she still didn't know how to dress.

Robert asked her if she liked Mexican food and hoped she said yes because he had made reservations at his favorite Mexican food restaurant. She did.

"You look nice," Robert told her as he pulled out of his parking spot.

"So do you!" Louise said with emphasis. She was thinking that he really was handsome and wondered what he looked like in his dark blue LAPD uniform. Oddly, her experience hadn't prejudiced her against police officers. She had had two drinks before he picked her up and was more conversational than normal. She began to look forward to getting dinner over with.

They ordered margaritas and then dinner. Louise ordered two tacos. Robert ordered an enchilada dinner. They made small talk over dinner and found out that they had a mutual friend at UCLA, the person who threw the party where they had met. Robert had attended UCLA earlier but never graduated. They grew silent as they ate their dinner. After dinner, Louise ordered a vodka tonic and Robert ordered a tap beer. Louise was beginning to feel a little better.

"You're dying to ask me aren't you," Louise said, taking a sip of her drink.

Robert knew exactly what she meant but, as a matter of fact, his mind was wandering and he was thinking of problems he was having with his divorce. He and his wife had no children but she was asking alimony. Robert didn't feel he owed her anything.

His thoughts came back to the present and he asked her, "Did you do it?"

"No, I did not. Now that's out of the way and I don't want to discuss it ever again," she said with a tone that suggested a plea.

"I'm glad you didn't and I'm glad that's out of the way!" Actually, he didn't believe her and he held on to his belief that she was a third victim of George Rector Gollum's avarice and brutality. He had been a cop for a while and he saw many situations where con men convinced otherwise good people into doing something that was bad and totally against their nature. Robert had followed the trial and read columnists' stories of how she was an unwanted, unloved and emotionally neglected child. His childhood had been just the opposite and he realized how important a good family life had been to him back in his home state of Nebraska.

It was only 8:00 PM when they finished dinner and they went to a local bar where he knew Louise would be able to get a drink. She looked much older than nineteen. It was what they call a cop watering hole. He asked if she was OK with it and she confessed that she actually had a viable ID making her twenty one and used it regularly.

"OK, then. Get ready to see the other side; shuffle board, pool and cheap beer...you can also get a vodka tonic but you better call your brand because if you don't you will get potato juice."

"I'm excited." she lied. "This is my most daring adventure since my first day in class in a public school!" She was not excited but she was apprehensive. With all the cops that would likely to be inside, and drinking, she worried about identification and crude remarks. She knew she had to face the world sooner or later. She was not asked to leave the Manhattan Street home of the Jungquists but it had grown uncomfortable. Neither Marjorie nor Uncle Fred had called her or visited her since she moved into a slightly upscale apartment in the same general neighborhood. Her Uncle Emmanuel and Uncle Fred's daughter Yvonne, along with her husband, who had testified against her and Bud, had not spoken to her since the verdict was read.

The bar was large with a small dance area, a pool room and two shuffle boards. Fortunately, it was dark. Several cops called a greeting and Robert introduced her to them as Louise. No one recognized her, of if they did, they didn't comment. She was thinking, "Maybe cops have more class than I thought," thinking of the guard who had befriended her and Bud and betrayed them with the letters.

They listened to some popular music on the juke box, passed some comment with some of Robert's friends who all treated her like a long lost friend, making faux suggestive comments to her, as cops and other blue collar workers always do. Robert sipped his beer and she put away two Vodka and tonics. She was obviously not a novice drinker. Robert was a cop and wanted to stay legally sober. That was easier in 1948 than it is today.

They left at 9:30 at her suggestion and went to her apartment.

She was getting more and more apprehensive as they approached her home. She lived about five miles away and the Friday night traffic slowed them down and they were in her apartment just before 10:00. She had bought some expensive foreign beer in anticipation of his being there and she brought one for him and one for her. By now, she was sure it was going to happen and was beginning to feel sensual. Making love was the one thing she did well. Although Bud had been her first and only lover, she felt more confident here with Robert than anywhere else she had been since the trial. When she was making love, she didn't see Bud and she didn't see the blood coming out of her mother's crushed skull. She knew the image would return but she was enjoying the respite and she was grateful to Robert for the interlude.

She asked him to spend the night and since he didn't have to work the next day, he agreed. He really didn't want to drive with that much liquor in his system. Although he realized he was with a less than beautiful girl, he was comfortable. He had his fill of the arrogance of a beautiful woman.

They had breakfast together and he went home to get some sleep. They agreed to see each other the following Friday. As it turned out, he called her the next day and he met her at her apartment with some takeout Chinese. Louise couldn't shake the image of seeing her mother murdered and her forced indifference, almost exuberance, in the days immediately following the murder. She began to realize she never would and welcomed what little relief she found. Robert gave her that brief break; for now, anyway.

They decided that he would move in with her and get married when his divorce was final. But to keep the department off his back, he would have to keep his apartment. He decided to sublet it and keep his address intact. She still felt, in the back of her mind, that he was attracted to her because of her money…which she didn't actually have yet and was not sure how much it was…but enjoyed his company. Unlike Bud, he had a job, a career and expected to work. Robert didn't love her but he had to admit that sex with her was much better than with his ex-wife and he enjoyed her glibness and repartee. She was an intelligent woman. His ex-wife was not so bright and couldn't tell a double entendre from a news report. He expected to keep working. He loved being a cop but he had to admit that the prospect of marrying into some serious money gave him a bit of a positive glow.

On July 15, 1948, Louise found out that the amount of her inheritance after her attorneys were paid was $309,977; far less than the millions that she and Bud had anticipated. Still, by today's prices that was a healthy sum of money. Successful businesses were started with less. A family could retire comfortably with it in 1948. Louise's problem was that in his wisdom, Walter held the money from her through his will until her twenty first birthday, April 30, 1950. She had to live off the interest, about $800 a month until then. To put it in perspective, skilled workers in the construction trades were supporting families on $600 a month. Louise would not starve.

At Robert's birthday party on August 22, his twenty eighth birthday, she announced that they were going to get married when his divorce was final in July of next year. The story was carried in the local papers and when asked, Robert replied that he intended to support them on his salary. The announcement attracted a lot of attention on the Los Angeles Police Department. His was the hottest topic of gossip for a while. To a man, or woman, members of the PD thought Louise was a murderess. Ray Pinker, the Criminal Identification officer who did the blood workup for the Orange County Sheriff's Department and testified at the trial, contacted Robert. Robert knew of Pinker but Pinker had never heard of Robert before the marriage announcement. Cops, for the most part, are protective of each other. Pinker met him after he got off his shift one day, introduced himself and asked him to join him for a cup of coffee. Robert recognized him and knew exactly what he was going to say but agreed to join him. They went into the officers' lounge. Pinker had been on the department for fifteen years and had a degree in chemistry. He was a big guy who looked more like a bouncer than a chemist.

He got to the point, "I don't know you, Robert, and you don't know me, but we are on the Los Angeles Police Department and that gives me an interest in your well-being. I have more experience than you, more time on the PD and more time on this earth. I also know much more than you about that trial and about your fiancée. She is a cold blooded murderess. There is no doubt about it. Don't do this."

Robert was just a little irritated by what he considered a condescending attitude but took a sip of his coffee and reflected while he adjusted his attitude for his response.

"Ray, I appreciate your concern for me. I really do. I'm sure you are sincere. I followed the case daily and I know Louise better than you."

"Have you asked her straight up if she did it?" Pinker bluntly suggested.

Robert answered, "As a matter of fact, I have, and she told me she didn't kill her parents. She also said that was the last time she was going to discuss it with me and I have never brought it up again."

Robert saw that Pinker was going to reply, was sure of what he was going to say and beat him to the pulpit.

"Look, Ray, I'm not a kid. I don't have your experience – in life or on the PD – but I have been around the block a few times. I was in the war and I've seen my share of carnage as a cop. I know that Louise was there when Bud Gollum killed her parents and that she gave her approval. But I think she was a victim of Gollum's greed and manipulation. I know she is going through hell right now."

Ray looked at Robert and asked bluntly, "Robert, do you love her?"

Robert was annoyed but answered, "I don't know. Does anyone really know for sure? All I know is, I enjoy being with her and I feel sorry for her."

Ray was about to make the obvious reply that sympathy was not a good foundation for marriage but realized how trite it would sound and how useless it would be, and said simply, "OK, Robert, I feel like I have given you the best advice I could. I hope you're not offended. I wish you the very best."

He took a last sip of his coffee, looked at his watch, held out his hand which Robert took, and left.

Louise and Robert continued living together semi secretly and she quit going to school. Her nightmares continued as did her drinking.

On June 30, 1949, they took out their marriage license with the press present. When asked by reporters, he told them that he intended to support himself and his wife on his policeman's salary. They were married the following day, Friday, July 1, 1949 at the First Christian Church.

It was a quiet wedding. Louise and Robert tried to keep it out of the papers. Most of the people who attended were friends of Robert's from the LAPD. Very few of the Jungquists attended. Louise had made an overture to her mother's family to attend the wedding. The Jungquists were not hostile to her but most of them had become reconciled to the fact that she was complicit in her mother's murder. The consensus had become firmer in the belief that Bud used her.

She talked to her Uncle Fred and Uncle Emmanuel. Fred had a legitimate prior commitment and couldn't attend. Both he and Emmanuel had testified against her but still felt a kinship. Louise pleaded with Emmanuel. "Uncle Manny, I have no one to give me away."

"That's because your boyfriend murdered your father," Emmanuel replied coldly.

"That's not so, Uncle Manny, he, we were found not guilty in a fair trial." Louise said with a pleading tone.

"The trial was **not** fair." Emmanuel retorted. "No one else could have done it. Your father had no reason to consider suicide. His business was doing well. Look, Louise, the family knows that you were under the influence of Bud. You need to acknowledge that, ask forgiveness from God and the family and start to heal. Alcohol will not change anything."

"Please, Uncle Manny." Louise started to sob which was rare for her. Emmanuel had never seen this before and it softened him.

"All right, Louise I will walk you to the altar but I will not give you away, only your father could do that."

Louise walked into the church on the arm of her uncle Emmanuel, but he did not stay at the altar for the wedding. She decided then that after she gained control over her inheritance on her twenty first birthday, to distance herself from her family. Her uncles Fred and Manny were her personal guardians but exercised no control over her activities. She had never been close to them anyway. She was the ugly stepdaughter to them. It was the most impossible situation a family could be in. They were a close family. They knew Louise was guilty, at least in abetting the crime, and they knew that she knew. Dialogue gradually went away between her and the rest of the family, as did the contact.

Louise had commented to the press that there would be no honeymoon but that was just to keep the press away. Robert had to wait a few days for his scheduled vacation and they went to a mountain resort without telling anyone where they would be.

They returned from their honeymoon in the middle of August and Robert returned to work at the police department. He worked the swing shift

– 4:00 PM to midnight. When he got home, he usually found Louise drunk. The excitement of the marriage and having a man in her life did nothing to remove the demons – the constant image of Bud crushing her mother's skull.

Their life grew into a routine. She got drunk every day alone and they got drunk together on his days off. Two people with a drinking problem are a recipe for a lot of drunkenness. Louise was Robert's third wife. Outside of her husband, who she continued to love, Louise had no social life. On his days off, they would party with his friends on the department, usually at a house party but sometimes at the local watering hole after dinner.

The weeks rolled into months and soon the day they had been waiting for arrived; April 30, 1950, Louise's twenty first birthday. She inherited nearly $310,000 dollars and became an adult. The money was hers with which to do whatever she wanted. The only person who welcomed it more than Louise was Robert who had no intentions of ever drawing a pension from the Los Angeles Police Department. He had failed the sergeant's exam twice and was not a particularly good cop. He had peter principled at the patrolman's level. To put her inheritance in perspective, although it was less than she and Bud had anticipated when Bud bludgeoned her mother and father to death and blew up the boat:

The average annual income in 1950 was around $3,300 per year.
The average annual income in the US in 2011 is $42,000.
The inheritance was 94 times average annual American income.
That equates to over $3,948,000 today.
The Thompsons were wealthy by today's standard.

He had been preparing Louise for leaving the department by constantly complaining about the hours, poor supervisors and low pay. She was sympathetic. He suggested that they buy a cocktail lounge and operate it themselves. She was receptive. She hated the lonely hours when he was working and she sat alone in the apartment watching soap operas or listening to music and drinking as the demons danced in her brain. Maybe owning a business would obscure the guilt that was driving her insane.

Their search began before her birthday. Louise suggested that rather than looking in the ads in the paper for a bar for sale, it would be wiser to find one that was doing well and make an offer. She wisely reasoned that it would be better to pay more for one that was succeeding than to pay less for one that was failing. On May 2, 1950, the money was in Louise's hands and in June they purchased a bar; they bought the local police watering hole for $60,000. Robert used his retirement funds to pay half.

The business did well. Income from the bar, after all expenses were paid, averaged three times what Robert had been making as a patrolman on the LAPD. Robert was the primary bartender and Louise kept the books and inventory. They did some things to increase business and it worked. They made it more female friendly. The presence of a handsome bartender during prime hours was no small contributor.

Robert was able to keep his drinking under control but Louise was not. She spent more and more time at home in a drunken stupor or passed out and less and less time helping Robert. He didn't really need her. Their relationship became more and more marginalized. Robert actually preferred it when she was not around.

Louise noticed that he was friendlier with the female customers than he was the males and frequently commented on it. She was growing more and more jealous. But it didn't stop her from drinking; quite the contrary. One evening, or early morning, after closing, Louise came by and found him in a compromising position with a female customer in the office behind the bar. Louise walked out on him. He didn't know where she was for a week. She had taken a plane to Las Vegas and spent the week at one of the casinos.

Robert continued to keep the customers happy and Louise left him for the fourth and final time on September 7, 1950. She was expecting a child in January at the time. They made an out of court settlement. The divorce became final in 1952 and Louise got custody of their son, Jimmy,[20] who was born in December of 1950. Robert kept the bar and there is no record of his activities after the divorce.

Louise moved to Las Vegas to escape her notoriety shortly after her son was born. She also moved to get away from the discomfort of knowing her family, the Jungquists, had tacitly if not openly shunned her. She was also conscious and ashamed of her excessive drinking and decided it would be less painful if she drank in anonymity. She believed Las Vegas would provide that seclusion. She had given up escaping the demons. It got worse if anything. It was taking more and more alcohol to put her to sleep and even then she saw Bud crushing her mother's skull with a hammer. Her normal

---

20 Not his real name as he is still living.

pattern was to have dinner after a few vodka tonics and then wash it down at a piano bar where she could listen to music in hopes of making her mind go blank. It only worked for a while and then she would retreat to her apartment where she would drink herself into oblivion.

Occasionally, she would make a connection and go home with them or take them home with her. She became able to function socially with a large amount of liquor in her system – as many alcoholics can. Her figure remained slender; she ate very little. She was never hungry. She still didn't like to dress provocatively but she did learn to divert attention away from the less attractive elements of her persona. She still enjoyed sex and she was good at it. She had a few regulars but assiduously avoided entanglements. The last thing she needed was another person after her money. She remained wealthy. She had no expensive habits and even as much as she drank she couldn't drink up the interest on her holdings. But whatever she did, wherever she went and with whomever she made love, she was always aware that the images, the demons, were out there just waiting to pounce.

She was on one of her outings in November of 1952 in a cocktail lounge off the strip celebrating her divorce from Robert becoming final. Louise Preferred drinking in the lounges away from the strip because of the easier parking and fewer people in the bar. She was always concerned with being recognized by some Los Angeles people. Most of the local drinkers, the ones who drank in the bars, also avoided the strip. She usually dropped Jimmy off at a baby sitter when she was out. Usually, she drank at home. Louise was approached by a young man who, ironically, recognized her from the trial and subsequent newspaper coverage. He was a Los Angeles transplant who had moved to Las Vegas a few years earlier because of his job as a sales representative for a sewing machine manufacturer. He had light brown hair, nearly blond, with blue eyes and a ruddy complexion. He wore his hair in a high pompadour which was popular in the fifties.

Louise was sitting alone in a booth at the rear of the bar.

"Hi, Louise," he greeted her.

Louise looked at him, thought he was a nice looking young man, and replied in a not unfriendly tone, "Do I know you"? She actually was not sure. She had met a lot of people recently who she didn't remember.

"I'm Albert Vander Meer,[21]" he volunteered, "people call me Al; and no we haven't met but I have seen you in Robert's lounge in Los Angeles. I had a drink in there once in a while. And, I don't want to bring up unpleasant memories but I also know you from the trial."

"And you think I have money!" Louise remarked somewhat sardonically.

"I know you do but that doesn't make you a bad person." Al replied, "I don't have any, so that makes us even, so do I buy you a drink or do you buy me one?"

"You buy me one. The rumors about my money are false," Louise quipped, "and I'm sure you have enough money to buy me a drink!"

"Only if I can share your booth."

"That sounds reasonable please sit down, Al," Louise said.

The two had several drinks together and Louise was captivated by his humor and candor. She had had several sexual encounters since divorcing Robert but they were casual and motivated by her over active libido and the temporary escape from the deadly haunting images that sex provided. She always knew that escape was only temporary and that made her increasingly desperate. Louise was truly tormented.

They closed the evening by going to Louise's apartment. They had a drink there and finished off the evening with sex that this time, for Louise, didn't feel perfunctory. Louise was still homely, of course, and she was aware of it and realized that there was always the probability that any interest in her beyond easy sex was because of her money. This put her constantly on defense and she assiduously avoided emotional entanglements. She had been burned immeasurably by her initiator, Bud, and to some extent by Robert, the father of Jimmy. She was also aware that she could attract men sexually and please them as she pleased herself. Alcohol and sex and the omnipresent demons had become her life. In her rare sober moments, she tried to spend time with her infant son not wanting him to feel toward her as she had toward the parents she had aided Bud in murdering.

Al was different; at least he succeeded in making her think so. They became regular, skipped the bar scene and usually spent the evenings at his apartment leaving Jimmy with the baby sitter. On May 1st, 1953, the couple was married in the St. Paul Lutheran Independent church by Reverent

---

21 Albert Vander Meer is a fictitious character as is the depiction of his relationship to Louise.

Thomas J. Daly. Al continued to work but talked Louise into buying a home where "Jimmy would have a better environment."

This began the final phase of Louise's self-destruction. Louise tried to be a good mother. She genuinely loved her son who was the only glimmer of normalcy in her convoluted life of drunken stupor.

On August 8, 1955, she was arrested for drunk driving when she turned over her car with Jimmy in the car. Fortunately, he was not hurt. Fortunately, or unfortunately for her, Louise was not hurt either but she did have to pay a $500 fine. Al had to bail her out and was enraged. Al was a drinker but managed it better than Louise and he became increasingly impatient with her drunkenness. She continued to drink and her health, mentally and physically, deteriorated. The couple grew more extravagant in buying material things and living beyond his income. She tried several times for rehabilitation but she refused to give up the temporary respite from the demons that her drunkenness provided and they were futile.

Her slippery slope became a steep decline and on August 24, 1965, she went to her bedroom with a loaded .22 rifle and two bottles of Vodka. Her apparent intention was to anesthetize herself with the vodka and kill herself with the rifle. The gun became unnecessary; the alcohol killed her. Her son and Al found her nude body and called the police. She had bruises all over her body which Al passed off to the police as being due to her drinking and constantly falling down.

Louise's mortal torment was over. Now she was in the hands of God.

On January 25, 1966, the court awarded Louise's son Jimmy Thompson what remained of her inheritance. Al had whittled it down to $28,845. The money was placed in a trust for him until his twenty first birthday. Al kept Jimmy around with hopes of getting some of the money but when he turned twenty one, Jimmy took the money and ran. He retreated to a remote area of another state where he would be away from the Overells, Gollums, Thompsons, and Vander Meers.

Bud's situation was different than Louise's. Bud felt no guilt and had no remorse. He felt denied because his plot did not work out for him. The Hare Psychopathy Checklist-Revised (PCL-R) is a diagnostic tool used to rate a person's psychopathic or antisocial tendencies.[22] It lists the following 20 traits of the psychopathic character:

---

22 http://www.minddisorders.com/Flu-Inv/Hare-Psychopathy-Checklist.html

Glib and superficial charm
Grandiose (exaggeratedly high) estimation of self
Need for stimulation
Pathological lying
Cunning and manipulativeness
Lack of remorse or guilt
Shallow affect (superficial emotional responsiveness)
Callousness and lack of empathy
Parasitic lifestyle
Poor behavioral controls
Sexual promiscuity
Early behavior problems
Lack of realistic long-term goals
Impulsivity
Irresponsibility
Failure to accept responsibility for own actions
Many short-term marital relationships
Juvenile delinquency
Revocation of conditional release
Criminal versatility
Reviewing George Rector Gollum's life shows nearly all of these traits.

Theodore Millon identified five subtypes of antisocial behavior.[23] Any anti-social individual may exhibit none, one or more than one of them. Bud Gol-lum exhibits the following one: Covetous antisocial - where individuals feel that life has not given them their due. It has been described as follows:

Aggrandizement, the desire to possess and dominate, is seen in a distilled form. These individuals feel that life has not given them their "due"; they have been deprived of their rightful amount of love, support, or material reward; and others have received more than their share. Jealous of those who have received the bounty of a good life, they are driven by an envious desire for retribution to take what destiny has refused them. Whether through deceit or destruction, their goal is compensation for the emp-

---

23 http://en.wikipedia.org/wiki/Antisocial_personality_disorder#Millon.27s_subtypes

tiness of life, rationalized by the assertion that they alone can restore the imbalance fated to them. Seething with anger and resentment, their greatest pleasure lies in taking control of the property and possessions of others. Some are overtly criminal. Many possess an enormous drive for revenge, manipulating others like pawns in a power game.

Regardless of their success, however, covetous antisocials usually remain insecure about their power and status, never feeling that they've been compensated for life's impoverishments. Ever jealous and envious, pushy and greedy, they may make ostentatious or wasteful displays of mate-rialism and conspicuous consumption such as buying exotic cars, man-sions, and elaborate jewelry as a means of exhibiting their power and achievements to others. Most feel a deep sense of emptiness; juxtaposed with vague images of how different life might have been had opportu-nity blessed them, as it has so many others. Some are simple thieves, while others become manipulative entrepreneurs who exploit people as objects to satisfy their desires. Although they have little compassion for or guilt about the effects of their behavior, they never feel that they have acquired quite enough, never achieve a sense of contentment, and feel unfulfilled regardless of their successes, remaining forever dissatisfied and insatiable.[24]

Bud's path to destruction or inevitable retribution, as it were, was not the result of conscience or feelings of guilt. It was the natural result of what he was and not being very good at it.

After the trial and the breakup, he was lost. Having been thwarted in obtaining, through the murders, what he considered to be rightfully his, he found himself without any goals or prospects. The one big opportunity that fate had seemed to offer him, the Overell fortune through marriage to Lou-ise, had gone by the wayside. Not only had the fortune he sought turned out to be less than he had believed, but he was cast aside by someone whom he had thought was inferior and under his spell.

To count his losses and lick his wounds, he enrolled in classes at UCLA in hopes of living off the Stomels or Rectors but Bud had closed all doors

---

24 Anon

that had been opened to him. His grandparents, longtime friends of his victims, though they ostensibly supported him during the trial and tried to tell themselves that Louise was the engineer of the plot, didn't really believe it and told him it was time for him to move on and make a life for himself. His stepfather, Dr. Stomel, saw through him from the beginning and over the objections of his wife, Wilhelmina, Bud's mother, refused any support. Bud's mother and sister, Wilafred, were virtually the only two people in the world who stood by him.

Bud got a cheap apartment and applied for education benefits under the GI Bill Of Rights. The government paid the tuition to the veteran's school of choice and provided approximately $100 a month living expenses. It made for a tight budget and the GI's usually had to augment their stipends with work. He was also uncomfortable with all the notoriety that the murder trial had given him. He got tired of proclaiming his innocence and enduring the anger displayed by many who felt he had gotten away with killing two people.

He stayed in school at UCLA until the summer of 1949, working part time in various jobs. It was hard for him to find dates. He was a nice looking young man with a scholarly appearance but his name scared people off. He had a strong sexual appetite and his time with Louise spoiled him for "normal" sex. His social awkwardness and his propensity for trying to present himself as an intellectual impressed some for a while but the impression was fleeting and some people considered him shallow and insincere. His sexual encounters were few and were usually what is considered one night stands or with prostitutes.

He decided to move on. He answered an ad and was hired by a traveling carnival that was operating at the time in the Los Angeles area. He was hired as a general laborer but his college experience and the general skills he picked up in the Navy and in his odd jobs put him well above most of the carnival roustabouts and he was soon made an assistant to the manager, keeping books and supervising some of the operations. Bud was temporarily contented with his work and made himself believe that he could climb to the top of the operation and take over as manager.

He met a young woman who was a daredevil motorcycle rider. She was very attractive; tall with an athletic figure. She had dark hair and large brown eyes. Bud was captivated. Her name was Shirley. She had just turned twenty one years old and they threw an impromptu birthday party for her after they had just sat up to start a stay in a small town in Florida. Bud was not a heavy drinker but he occasionally had a beer. As he was walking to get himself a beer, he passed by Shirley and asked her if she would like one.

"Sure," Shirley answered, "it's my twenty first birthday and I can drink legally now." Not that it ever made a difference," she quipped with a chuckle. "You're the new guy that joined up in LA, aren't you."

"That's me," he answered.

"What's your name?"

"George, but people call me Bud, and I know your name. You're the star of the show!" Shirley was, indeed, the star of the show. She rode a motor cycle in a barrel-shaped wooden cylinder, thirty six feet in diameter, climbing up the wall, doing handstands on the bike, riding backward, doing wheelies and other incredible feats of skill and daring.

"Glad to meet you, Bud, you're kind of cute," she giggled starting to feel the effects of the alcohol.

Bud was glad she hadn't asked his last name but reasoned that she probably wouldn't recognize it anyway. It had been over two years and people in carnivals aren't usually too aware of what's going on in the news.

"So are you," he replied.

She sat down with him and they had two more beers making small talk. He told her about his experience in combat in the Navy and she told him how she had been born in Minnesota and learned how to ride the motorcycle from her big brother. She was a natural, soon surpassing her brother in skill. She was absolutely fearless. Shirley was an athlete. Unfortunately, in the forties female athletes were not important. When she got out of high school, she decided to hone her skills and have a go at riding for money. She didn't want to do it forever but thought it would be fun for a while. She checked the papers and found an ad for a stunt motorcycle rider. The previous rider had decided to retire. She answered the ad and was hired. She was billed as the only female motorcycle stunt rider in the world; probably not true, but there weren't many.

After a while he suggested that they go into town and get something to eat. Bud didn't have a car, most of the carnival workers didn't. They traveled with the carnival vehicles.

"How are we going to get there?" Shirley asked. "Wanna ride on the motorcycle with me?" She was a little tipsy.

"Uhh, probably not a good idea," he replied. "I can take one of the company pickups."

"OK, coward," she said with mock disdain.

They drove the few miles to town and went to a diner. As they sat down, Bud realized that the last time he had eaten in a diner with a date was on March 15, 1947, while they were waiting for the dynamite to explode on the Mary E and hide his crime. He withdrew into his thoughts briefly and indulged into self-pity and was piqued at his bad luck. He still blamed misfortune for his ineptitude and lack of planning. He shrugged his shoulders and thought, "Oh well, the bitch didn't' have any money anyway."

"What are you thinking about, big guy?" Shirley asked playfully, "how in the hell you ever ended up keeping books in a carnival?"

Bud shrugged his shoulders. "It's a living," he replied with a smile.

"Sorry you're here instead of back in LA?"

"This isn't so bad," he lied, "and I've never liked Los Angeles that much except that it's by the ocean and I love sailing." Actually, he was getting warmed up to the possibilities with this beautiful young girl. She was much more attractive than Louise and probably has as much money, he thought sardonically.

"You like to sail, do you, I still don't understand how they get a boat to go south when the winds blowing north." I used to watch them on the lakes in Minnesota.

They ordered hamburgers and French fries and cokes and continued their small talk.

When they finished and got in the pickup, Shirley moved close to him and asked, "Do you have any beer in your trailer?" Shirley had been somewhat active, sexually, in high school and was not coy.

Bud didn't. He was not much of a drinker. "I will when we get there," he replied with more satire than he normally was able to muster.

He stopped and picked up a six-pack but they never drank it. Bud was incapable of selfless love but in the morning, he came closer than he ever had. He found himself trying to figure out a way to harness her talent into a better market than a carnival. They kept their affair secret because the carnival manager forbade fraternization between the staff. He had seen too many problems. There were a couple of married workers but they had been a couple when he hired them.

Bud decided that he was valuable enough to the operation that if he were married to Shirley, the manager might let it go. He really wanted the relationship and saw Shirley as a low grade security blanket. In the next town, they found a justice of the peace and got married. When Harvey, the manager, an older guy, found out, he was enraged. He was the only one who knew Bud's background and he felt a fatherly responsibility for Shirley. He had met her father. Bud was fired on the spot and he told Shirley about the Newport Beach murders and the trial. She was horrified. Bud was given two weeks' pay and left stranded in the town. Shirley filed for an annulment claiming that the marriage had never been consummated

Bud was enraged but helpless. He was a big man; Harvey was a gnarled little man with a quick temper and a biting profane tongue. Bud was offended by Harvey's insults and considered hurting him but decided against it. He had never had a fight in his life. He was naturally strong but had no athletic ability. The closest to a fight he had ever had was when he crushed Walter's skull with the end of a pipe. As the carnival left him in town, he wanted to do that. This was just another of the bad luck events that was destined to be Bud's future.

He was left with just a little over $150 in his pocket and no car. He called his sister, Pete, who was sympathetic but had no money. She was living with her mother and Dr. Stomel and Dr. Stomel was not thrilled with having Pete living with them while she went to school. He talked to his mother the next day and she agreed to send him $50. He felt betrayed but he took the money. He got a room in a cheap hotel and a job stocking the shelves in a local market. He was feeling more and more victimized by fate. Why did the damned dynamite not explode as he planned, he kept thinking. They wouldn't have been arrested, the lurid notes wouldn't have happened, he would be living with Louise at 607 Los Robles, in Flintridge and having wild sex like "the old days." Even if the fortune was not as much as he expected, it was better than living in a room with a bed, toilet, shower and dresser; and stocking boxes at a cheap market in Florida beach town.

He worked there for a few months, looking for a way out and blaming everyone else for his predicament. The fact that he had murdered two people and drug a malleable young woman into his bloody scheme seldom entered his mind. He was having a dinner at the local diner sitting at the counter next to a man in a cheap suit and tie. The guy was tall and emaciated looking with a pock marked face and a mustache that was too big for his face. He introduced himself as Tony and struck up a conversation with Bud who was not really interested in conversation…particularly with this seedy looking character. In the conversation, Bud mentioned casually that he was trying to get back to Los Angeles. Tony looked at him for a second and told him that he was a foreign car broker and was looking for someone to drive an imported car to a customer in Charleston, South Carolina. Bud was suspicious.

"Why don't you drive it up there?" he asked.

"I'm in the car import business, not the driving business," he replied with a smile. "I have a regular driver but he just got married and is on his honeymoon. I can't wait a week until he comes home. Look, Tony continued, if you drive it up there, I'll give you $50 and a bus ticket on Greyhound from Charleston to Los Angeles."

Bud was still suspicious. What had occurred to him was the foreign car smuggling business that he knew existed where people would save a lot of money on avoiding the import tax. He asked Tony if that was the deal and Tony didn't reply. He looked at him for a few seconds and as he put some money on the counter and started to leave, asked, "Do you want the job or not. Or do you prefer staying in this moldy town?"

Bud told him he would do it and asked him where the car was and when did he want him to leave. Tony told him, "Be here at 8:00 AM tomorrow and I'll give you the keys, the money and a Greyhound bus ticket." Bud met him in the morning as directed and left immediately. Although he knew he was probably involved in something illegal, he needed to get back to Los Angeles. What he didn't know was that the car was stolen and was being taken to Charleston to a chop shop where the car would be dismantled and sold as parts. He planned to drive to Charleston that day, deliver it early in the morning and be on the bus to Los Angeles tomorrow.

In the afternoon, he was stopped by a South Carolina State Trooper and arrested for car theft. The car had been reported stolen in Florida earlier that day. A month later, Bud pled guilty in federal court in Savanna, Georgia, on a plea bargain, cooperating with the police in their investigation of the chop shop operation. On February 24, 1950, he was sentenced to a year in federal prison and was released in three months. The bus ticket which had been seized as evidence was returned to him and he returned to Los Angeles, arriving, ironically, on Louise's twenty first birthday. When he read about her getting control over her $310,000 inheritance and being married to the Los Angeles policeman, Bud, once again, cursed his bad luck on March 15, 1947, when the dynamite never exploded as he had planned. He could be celebrating with Louise instead of living in a cheap apartment looking for a job.

He got in touch with his mother and his sister, Pete, ostensibly to let them know he was OK but mostly to ask for help. He also contacted his grandfather, George Rector. His grandmother, Minnie, had passed away in 1948, a year after the trial. The grandfather had softened somewhat but he was still embarrassed and ashamed of his grandson. He was still sure he had been guilty but he had been influenced by Wilhelmina who had convinced herself that Bud was innocent and tried to convince her father that if Bud had been involved, he was pulled into it by Louise. He wanted to believe it but couldn't get past the indisputable fact that a good man can't be talked into doing something as heinous as killing two people.

George was an old construction man and had been very successful. He had started from the bottom and had worked with the tools and believed that hard work would be rewarded. Even though he saw through Bud, he was flesh and blood and he wanted no more harm to come to him. He was a religious man and knew that Bud's worst punishment wouldn't come in this life. He was eighty years old but kept up with current events and told Bud that the future would involve war preparation. He gave Bud $500 and encouraged him to enroll in training courses that would provide him with marketable skills.

Bud took his grandfather's advice and, renewing his GI Bill rights, enrolled in a trade school studying electronics, thinking satirically to himself that if he had done it three years ago, he would have known how to make an explosion and he wouldn't have to be going to school now. Bud realized that all the doors to easy living had been closed and for the first time in his life was determined to make a life on his own. He got an apartment close by the Stomels and his mother surreptitiously gave him some money each month but even with the government aid it was hard paying the rent and other bills.

Pete and Bud's mother approached Dr. Stomel about Bud staying with them until he got back on his feet. "Out of the question," Dr. Stomel shouted in his Russian accent, "we would have to stay awake every night worrying about him breaking our skulls with a hammer!" He had added the explanation as a way to hurt his wife and stepdaughter. He had never liked any of the Rectors or their friends the Overells.

When Wilhelmina told her father what the doctor had said, it infuriated him. Even though he felt his grandson had done the murder, it bothered him that Joseph, who he had never liked, would be so openly savage in his accusation. "Why don't you and George just move in with me and ditch that stupid Russian son of a bitch."

"I can't do that, Dad. Don't ask me why. I've had one divorce and can't handle another one," she answered; "how about if just George moves in with you. I know you get lonesome in this big house with Mom gone."

The old man thought about it a while, softened his attitude and said, "Well, OK, for a while until he finishes his class. We'll see how it goes."

Dr. Stomel and Wilhelmina never had a good marriage. His practice earned a good income but he lived very frugally; more frugally than his wife felt was necessary. He resented the opulence of the Rectors and Overells and their conspicuous consumption. He kept a close rein on the budget but she planned to keep helping Bud out a little whether he liked it or not.

Bud's new found determination made his mother and sister, the only two friends he had in the world, very happy. He went to school through the summer and when he graduated, the school found him a job with a firm that manufactured nuclear controls. It was a good job and it paid fairly well and provided him with health insurance and social security benefits. To his amazement, he began enjoying having a job and he earned several promotions. He moved into an apartment, bought a new car and started dressing well again. He was not a drinker and he didn't attend church so his social life was empty. He satisfied his libido with an occasional prostitute. He spent most of his holidays and weekends on the water sailing or just sitting around on the beach. He loved the sea and sometimes wondered why he didn't stay in the navy; but then remembered the letters from Louise and the promise of affluence that she offered.

He met Rose at work. She worked in the office at the plant. She was small and slender with soft blond hair that she wore parted on the side with loose waves not quite to her shoulders reminiscent of how Marilyn Monroe wore her hair. She had a coquettish demeanor and laughed easily. Bud never worked out. The only exercise he got was on his little one man rented sailboats but he had good eating habits and he maintained his weight very well. He looked good in his clothes. Rose was attracted to him.

They began eating together in the cafeteria and they established a natural rapport. She was not wealthy, not particularly sexy but, in her own way, appealing. Bud didn't really understand what was happening but he enjoyed just talking to her and looked forward to the lunch break. He was disinclined to have an office romance. He was afraid it might be awkward. The stinging rebuke he received when Harvey learned of his marriage to Shirley and the prison time that it led to was on the back of his mind. Also, he was sure that she was not aware of his history – the murder trial and his arrest for car theft and incarceration. Strangely, in his distorted sense of propriety, he was more ashamed of that, an unfortunate incident in which he was truly a victim, or near victim, than of the murders that sometimes he let himself believe he did not really do. He also laid more and more of the blame on Louise's prodding.

He decided to move ahead but slowly. He invited her to dinner Friday night. He took her to a nice steak house and they had a quiet dinner and several glasses of wine. Rose was not much of a drinker either. He took her home without any romantic advances and asked her if she would like to do it again next Friday. She said yes. She became more and more attracted to him. They got into a brief routine of Friday night dates and lunches at work without any suggestion of sex or permanent relationships.

This went on for several months. Bud, as would most twenty five year old men who were dating a young woman steadily, became frustrated and wanted the relationship to escalate. He knew that she felt the same way. His main fear in elevating the level of involvement was what her reaction would be when and if she found out about his criminal past. He did not want a repeat of what he considered an over-reaction by his first wife when she found out that she may have married a murderer. He still considered her reaction irrational. He decided to tell Rose about his time in prison and his trial and acquittal on murder charges.

The next Friday, as he dropped her off at her home, he suggested they go somewhere the next day, maybe to the beach. She enthusiastically agreed.

She had also begun to wonder why the relationship hadn't moved further along. The next day he picked her up and they drove to Santa Monica. They had breakfast and moved out to the boardwalk to look at the ocean. He did not know where to start.

"So what do you want to talk about?" Rose asked him. "Bud, I've known from the beginning and I was wondering when you were going to tell me. As far as I'm concerned, a person is innocent until proven guilty and you were found not guilty."

Bud's immediate relief was short lived when he realized that she was talking about the trial and not his serving time in a federal prison.

"Rose, that's not all, that's not the worst. I served three months in federal prison for car theft shortly after the trial. I did not steal the car. I did not even know it was stolen. I was transporting it for someone who I thought was in the auto import business. I guess I knew it was not legitimate but I really needed the money, I was desperate."

Rose was silent for a while. She thought it strange that he thought that was more important as disclosure than the murder trial. If he was innocent both times, why was he more concerned about being accused of car theft than a double murder? She made a mental shoulder shrug and turned to him.

"So that's what has been standing between us, three months in a federal prison? You spent more time than that in the Orange County Jail," Rose remarked quizzically.

"But I was found innocent then," Bud explained. He did not understand her perplexity.

This was her first hint of his unusual attitude on social appearance and on morality. He thought it was socially more acceptable to be wrongly accused of murder than to be wrongly accused of car theft if he was punished for the lesser crime and not for the higher crime. She was actually relieved that the unseen barrier was gone and decided that she was nit picking.

"Bud," she said turning to him, "That is in the past. We can both put it behind us. I do not feel any different about you this morning than I did last night."

He felt the weight of the world lifted off his shoulders. They spent the rest of the morning making small talk and watching the people on the beach. They got back to her apartment, snacked a little, listened to some music and had sex for the first time. It was not wild like with Louise, and Rose did not have money, but he felt contented for the first time since the murders. For what may have been the first time in his life, Bud started a relationship without a selfish motive.

The couple continued to see each other regularly. They maintained separate apartments; in 1950, unmarried couples living together was not as socially accepted as today and Rose cared about appearances. In 1952, they got married. They both continued to work and with both incomes, they were quite comfortable. It began what was probably the longest and maybe the only normal period of Bud's life. He was never truly contented. He always believed that he had been deprived of the good life, the life of luxury, of yachts, the life of the idle rich which he imagined he had grown up in. But for ten years or more, he functioned as a day worker, a husband and briefly as a father.

In 1953, Rose gave birth to a daughter and in 1957, a son was born.[25] Like it or not, Bud had a family. It did not last long, however. Disharmony began to intrude in the marriage and in 1966, when the children were 13 and 9. Bud was dissatisfied with his work, being jealous of those who were promoted above him, and quit the job with the excuse that he no longer wanted to be involved in the war industry. Rose filed for divorce. Bud's mother, Wilhelmina Stomel, was widowed in 1962 and was very much involved with her grandchildren. Shortly after the death of her husband, she had moved to Mountain Ranch in Calaveras County. She felt a sense of freedom when Dr. Stomel died and she wanted to get out of the congestion and smog of Los Angeles. She had become very close to Rose and convinced her to move in with her up in the mountains.

Bud moved up north also, trying his hand for a few years in real estate in the mountain areas. He moved from place to place and had very little success. When his children graduated from high school, they went back to "civilization" to go to college with the help of grandma. Bud kept in touch with his children while they were living with his mother and when they left, he moved to Mountain Ranch to try his luck there. He had no success so decided to try his hand in the narcotics business. He learned how to grow marijuana and went into business. He did pretty well until he was arrested in 1984. There is no record of him serving any time although he told people he

---

25 The dates of their birth and their names are not given in respect for their privacy. They are both living at the time of this writing.

did. His mother died on January 20, 1986. Rose stayed in Mountain Ranch until 1992 when she moved to Palmdale California. She died there that year.

Bud continued moving around, trying to sell real estate and growing marijuana. Shortly after his mother died, he moved to Wasilla, Alaska, and then to Palmer. He gave up on real estate and concentrated on growing marijuana.

On January 5, 2006, 2 months before his eightieth birthday, he was arrested by the Alaska State Troopers in Palmer, Alaska, on four counts related to growing marijuana for sale. He pled guilty to one charge, a felony and spent some time in an Alaska prison. He told the investigating officers that he lived alone, his only income was social security and grew marijuana for income but he made it clear that he did not smoke it. Typical of his perspective on morality, in his eyes it was better to grow it so that others can smoke it than to use it yourself. He told them that he was paid $4000 a pound. He also told the investigating officer that in 2002, his home had been invaded by two guys posing as state trooper, who beat him, tied him up and robbed him. When Bud was booked for murder on March 19, 1947, he weighed 220, when booked on January 5, 2006, he weighed 230 pounds.

After he served his time, Bud moved back to Wasilla, a neighboring city, and his dead body was found there on February 25, 2009, three days before his eighty fourth birthday. It's not known how he died or how long he lied dead before his body was discovered. His death was not important enough to warrant an obituary in the local paper.

So the ill-fated bifurcated odyssey of the conspirators ended nearly fifty four years later in a shack in Wasilla, Alaska. Between the two of them they left a trail of broken hearts and wounded lives. The two families who had been close were driven apart and who knows how it affected the members within the families. Louise was tormented with guilt. Of the two, she was probably the least guilty. Bud probably was not affected by the guilt. He most likely blamed bad luck, Louise, or the intransigence of the Overells.

Ironically, the idyllic life of the idle rich that they thought surrounded them and was rightfully theirs was an illusion. What they had been surrounded by was the fruits of hard work. Walter's fortune did not lie in his bank account, it was in his ability to earn money and that died with him. In all probability, if the plot had gone as planned, Bud and Louise would have gone through the money in a very short time and the end probably the same.

5038 THE FARMERS AND MERCHANTS NATIONAL BANK
OF LOS ANGELES
OLDEST BANK IN SOUTHERN CALIFORNIA

CABLE ADDRESS
"FARMERBANK"

LOS ANGELES 54, CALIFORNIA

October 31, 1947

James A. Musick, Sheriff
Orange County Jail
Santa Ana, California

Attention: Capt. Thomas R. McGaff, Bureau of Records
and Identification.

Dear Sir: Re: Estates of Walter E. Overell
               and Beulah A. Overell, Deceased
               Our Nos. CE-2245 and CE-2246

We are enclosing for your files a certified copy
of an order dated October 30, 1947, by Hon. Judge Kenneth
E. Morrison to the effect that all articles of personal
property of every kind and nature shall be delivered to
this bank as Executor and that the "Mary E", paraphernalia,
and equipment shall be delivered to the Executor or to the
purchaser of the "Mary E".

For your information the "Mary E" has been sold
and the new owner's name is Jacquelyne J. Jervis of 5113
East 61st Street, Maywood, California; and she is entitled
to possession of the boat, paraphernalia, and equipment.

It will be appreciated if you will forward to
us by Parcel Post all other articles of personal property
belonging to either estate, including Mr. Overell's watch,
any jewelry, keys or personal papers.

Please accept our thanks for your splendid
cooperation.

Yours very truly,

Assistant Trust Officer

WFH:nb
Enc.
c.c: Jacquelyne J. Jervis
Refer reply to:
Mr. W. R. Holland

The silent witness to the murders, the Mary E, did not fare much better
than the two victims, perpetrators or the two families. On October 10, 1947,
Attorney General Fred M. Howser, in a letter to Farmers and Merchants'
Bank, granted release of the yacht Mary E, stating the case was closed; a

formal acknowledgement of the incredible miscarriage of justice. On October 31, the bank directed Sheriff Musick to deliver the boat to the purchaser, Jacquelyne J. Jervis. The reported sales price was $7000. It was put on display in Long Beach where it earned the new owners a reported $75,000 before it was again sold.

The boat was sold several times and changed its name to the Westerly. In February, 1960, it was boarded by members of the Los Angeles Police Department abortion squad and two aboard were arrested for performing abortion on the boat. Three others were arrested on shore. It was last known as the Wonderlust, a refurbished bachelor pad. In spite of it's hard times, it had outlasted most of those who made her famous.

Appendix

EDITED VERSION OF NOTES OR LETTERS

BETWEEN BUD AND LOUISE

Notes from Louise[26]

Hi Pops,

I haven't got enough paper to write you a nice letter. But tomorrow or the next day, I will try.

Give me a black eye, please, in our next conference. Putty, pretty please. Otto hasn't come up yet. Heck, I'm getting to the point where I would give anything, almost, to be with you.

I finished your blue socks and I'll try to have Otto give them and the purple ones to you. I miss you, Pops, so much. If only I were your wife. I know they'd let me keep my wedding ring on. That would be such a comfort.

What's this joke you cracked on Easter. All the girls were laughing, so I went up and they told me. Listen, Dope, I love those jokes.

------

26 These notes were gleaned from clippings from the newspaper and reproduced on the internet. Some of the type is inaccessible or illegible.

The next letter indicates that the families are entering the pretrial dialogue:[27]

THE RELATIVES ARE OK. RELAX. I'M ONLY WORRIED ABOUT THE VERDICT. And whether I can hold out missing you so. Darling, I've been trying to imagine life without you. It doesn't work. My Pops, I love you so much, you mean so much to me. We've got so many memories, and you're my Pops.

Darling, I miss you so much. I love you with all of me. I adore you. I worship you. You're my Pops. Thank your family for everything. I can't tell you how much I appreciate it.

Oh, darling why do I love you so much? Otto has just been here. He is positive we will get off. Oh darling, my wonderful Pops. I love you.

Darling I think of you as more than a presence. A power all enduring. And I've got you. Please, Pops, I've got you. And you've got me.

Louise Gives property into Bud's keeping.

Please, I Louise Overell, give into keeping of George Rector Gollum any money and property I receive in the course of my life under the two provisions, namely, 1. That he is never in my life unfaithful to me in word or deed, thought excluded, and 2. that he never leave me.

Being of harassed and miserable frame of mind but sane and loving only aforesaid G. R. G, I declare the following to be a free and voluntary declaration.

There, now, but I hope you'll always love me. Oh my darling. Oh my Pops Popsie darling, my beautiful, handsome, intelligent Pops. I adore you always eternally. I never want anything else but to be alone with you. Working for you.

Your slave, Louise.

Miss Overell threatens, in her next letter, to take an overdose of sleeping pills if Gollum ever ceased to love her.

---

27 Bold type at the left margin indicates comments from the newspaper accounts and sometimes authors comments.

Hi Popsie.

Gooten morgen. Comment allez vous? Wie gehst du? As soon as we are acquitted I will meet you at the telephone downstairs. I promise you that nothing will move me until you come along.

Pop, I'm out of my cell from 7AM til 9AM. Unfortunately, since I'm such a dangerous character, I have to have someone with me to make sure I don't fall down while taking a bath.

We can wash our sheets whenever we feel like it. Do you have mattresses? The day matron taught me how to play cribbage. I've got my glasses a long time ago, and I gave them to Wayne to get different rims for me. My interest for Spanish being downstairs, I don't study much, but if you want me to. Sure we can get candy bars if we want them. Don't eat too many. I'm rather busy all day so don't have much time to write. Did you get your knitting? You'd better. Please, Pops, get busy doing something. I don't know what the arrangement is down there but please keep busy.

–––––

Sleeping Pill threat by the girl.

Darling, my sweet wonderful Pops, I adore you. I'm so afraid you won't or don't love me. Darling, if that ever happens, I will take a overdose of sleeping pills.

I'm worried. If we don't get something new in tomorrow I'm going to be the only white girl here. Tell your family how much I appreciate their contributions to my welfare. I love you, I adore you, I dream of you every night. Oh Pops, never leave me, please never leave me, please please never leave me. Never love anyone else. I love you so tremendously.

Those (deleted) men. They just brought up a lot of mending.

What heat is on? Darling what are they doing to you? What's happening? Don't let them worry you. Please, Pops, everything will be alright. What heat? I sure wish you were here with me this second and millions of seconds to come.

I got the joke, dear. I'm really not too stupid. Well, you've got me for always. I love you so much. I will try to give you the sox as soon as pos-

sible. I love you. I adore you. You're my life. You're my life. You're what I live for. Yours always, Louise.

Miss Overell assures Gollum in her next letter that she will still want to marry him after the trial.

Hi stupe, Pops darling.

I sure miss you. I adore you. Otto tells me I won't want to marry you after the trial. So I bet him and I don't like to lose a bet.

The relatives, Margaret Yvonne and little Fred were here. They brought me a malt. Can you do leather tooling down there? Please, darling, do something.

I miss you so much. I adore you I dream of your beautiful big chest. Darling Pops, no one will ever have as beautiful a chest as you. Darling, I don't want any other man. The thought is revolting. I want you. There's much I want to tell you and there's not time nor space.

I miss you. I love you so much. Pops I don't care if you are after me for only my money, large laugh, or what else as long as I've got you, faithful, that's all I care about.

I miss you sweetheart, your mind and body. I love you. I adore you. I worship you. My Pops.

Pops, I've been hoping all day I'd get to see you but, so far, no go. Cuss words.

I'm so lonesome for you. My sweet Popsie, will I ever get over hating to think of any other man? I don't know how you feel but that's how I feel. Just a great big lonesomeness in all of me. Missing all of you so dreadfully. Loving you so much. Adoring and worshipping you. Wanting my Pops.

All I've got is you, Pops. You're my whole life. Darling, darling, please don't leave me, don't be unfaithful. Please don't stop loving me because as bad as I feel now I at least feel I have your love and that you can't get away or be unfaithful.

I love you Popsie darling, my wonderful, beautiful gorgeous Pops. My intelligent handsome Pops. Your loving gal, Louise

-----

Here Miss Overell repeatedly asks Gollum's promise to marry her. She is hopeful of acquittal.

Sunday

Hello Pops, darling: I'm still working hard on our hope chest. Would you still marry me if I were broke? Oh Pops, darling, please promise me you will marry me. Please, Pops, and stick to your promise. Please marry me please, Popsie, and stay with me. I know that we will be acquitted. Believe that.

Calls him "only interest in life."

Please marry me and don't leave, Pops. I miss you so much. I love you so much. I adore you. Oh Pops, I love you. I get to see you tomorrow at 10:30. Hooray! Oh Pops, please promise. I don't want anything else but you and I'm afraid I'll lose you. Darling, if you ever married someone else, I think that would be the worst thing that could happen to me. I hereby resolve to follow you go (inaccessible) toward you. It is sufficient to say that you are my whole and only interest in life, that you are my rock, the only thing I want when hurt or sick, happy or sad.

Popsie, I cannot lose you without losing myself. I cannot forget you. You are too important to me.

Never leave me. Never stop loving me. Marry me. *Darling, that is so much to ask yet I ask it of you because I love you so much, depend on you so terribly (I'm not much good at letter writing). Your ever loving, Louise.*

———

You know something? I love you. I adore you. Don't start edging for the door. My mind is made up. Excepting the proverbial other woman, I am out for you. I shall track you anywhere you go, including the mortuary. You see, young man, I am obstinate, I'm determined, I've resolved to have you come hell or high water, even both at once. And being as positive as I am of the acquittal, I am planning the trap. How to trap you into honoring and obeying until (?) do us part.

You see old chap, old chap, you're not an ordinary kind of man. (Time out while I tell you an incidental. You remember I told you I told one girl off? Well, she was just now playing checkers with another girl and made a bad play so she said I've just got half my mind on this game.

So brilliant me says sarcastically, "Oh giving it your full attention." So now we're speaking less than ever. We ignore each other. That is, she ignores me and I make fun of her. (More joy and happiness).

You're an uplifted human being. You're the most intelligent person I have ever heard of. Einstein was a moron compared to you. You're so sensible and omnipresent. All knowing, etc. And handsome, beautiful, magnificent, gorgeous.

Hello Poppa darling, it's Monday morning now. I finished the napkins. We've got a woman now who's been alternately sick or coughing ever since Saturday night. Oh Popsie sweet, I could just sit and look at you for hours. I adore you so much, I'd give almost anything…illegible…to hear a fortune teller say we were never going to be separated.

I love you so much, my darling Popsie.

I've been so busy all day. Its three now and I haven't been still three minutes. First the coffee can covers and then enlarging the cooks pants and patching them. Then the machine stuck due to too much stuck thread. Oh, Popsie, I've missed you so much and all of me misses you all the time.

Just received beautiful package from your parents. Thank them but please! No more yarn for a while. I've got needle point to do, embroidery, four and one half pairs of sox and a sweater. I'm so busy I can't go to sleep.

And I have millions of tomatoes to eat. Gosh, Pops, I love you. If it helps, never think that I won't love you always. Remember that I love you. All my attention is centered on you now and forever.

Does it help any to know that you're the only person that means anything to me and that you mean everything to me?

Nothing I do is without thinking of you somehow in connection with it. Everything I do makes me better and more worthy to be your wife. Darling, that will be my future, you willing.

I promise you that I will devote all my time and efforts into making you happy and satisfied. This separation makes me realize how wonderful you are, and makes me feel again that I am not good enough for you.

My darling Pops, how did I ever get you? I can't believe that I have such a man. Do I really have you? You know, don't you, that you have me?

Popsie, I miss you so much. I'm so lonely and miserable without you. I don't know what else to write. You write such beautiful letters and they say exactly how I feel towards you, that when it comes to writing to you, I can only copy one of yours.

———

I love you. I adore you and your teeth and your glasses, oh all of you. I miss you calling on the phone.

I miss being critical of you for being late. I miss Catalina and you being there. I miss from July fourth to March fourteenth so much. Oh, Pops, my darling Popsie, I love you with all my heart, mind and body. I love you, I adore you, I worship you, my darling Pops.

Oh, Pops, I miss you so much. I'm so afraid I'll never marry you. I'm afraid to leave you after we're acquitted. I'm afraid to get my stuff because you'll get or be gotten away. Pops. Pops. Oh Pops.

Pops, I can't explain how I feel towards you. It is sufficient to say that you are my whole and only interest in life, that you are my rock, the thing I want when hurt, or sad, happy or sick.

I cannot for... illegible... and says he is making a hurried trip to L.A. Well, tomorrow now I even put on stockings. Oh(deleted)_____but I happen to know that it is a really urgent trip. Dear Otto is making gains but I still want to see you.

———

More evidence of rift through family

I just got your nice angry letter. Oh, I adore you. I love you. I could never stop loving you and wanting to marry you.

I don't give one small——about the relatives. My greatest pleasure will be in telling them thanks folks and go to ——-and meet my husband, Mr. Gollum.

Please, Pops, you are more than just a man. You are part of me and I could never wound that part of me by thinking of………?

———

Notes from Bud. Louise is thinking of making bail.

Dearest Darling Louise. I love you my sweetheart. I love and adore you and miss and desire and want you.

We will be acquitted my darling. I hope we will be. I hope against hope that we will be found not guilty. With all my heart and all my love for you and yours for me, I hope the jury finds us not guilty. If otherwise, you know what will happen.

PS. Do you need some paper and pencils and envelopes?

You asked if I thought you should ask to get out on bail. THAT IS UP TO YOU! I am just selfish enough to tell you I don't want you to get out on bail. If you were out on bail, you would be with your relatives all the time. They would continually try to talk you out of loving me or marrying me. You are right in that you wouldn't get to see me or write to me. You would, though, have decent bed, good food, be able to do what you wanted to do.

———

Threat to kill any other man.

You undoubtedly would find some young man whom you could think of without hating and whom you wouldn't think was after your money. If YOU want to, get yourself bailed out. I don't want you to, though. I like to see you. I like to get those notes from you. Strangely enough, I just happen to love you.

Maybe you are just asking me to say I don't love you so you can feel free to do what your relatives ask.

Well, I am not going to do that. I love you. If I could see you maybe I could show you how much. I would never tell anyone I don't love you because that would be a lie and I've never lied to you. And I refuse to do so now. I LOVE YOU. I AM GOING TO MARRY YOU. IF YOU EVER MARRY ANYONE ELSE, I WILL KILL HIM. YOU CAN TAKE YOUR (deleted) MONEY AND THROW IT TO THE DOGS.

As I've said before, if you even so much as think (from letter or word) that your love for me is faltering, or turning toward someone else, we will leave then (even if I have to forcibly kidnap you.

I want you and I want you without any doubts on your mind. Damn your relatives and that fortune teller of yours and the matron and Mr. Jacobs. Damn the whole kit and caboodle of them.

I've made up my mind you want me to be one those "iron fists in a velvet glove deals". OK, you just watch out the glove doesn't come off and the fist bruise your tender skin.

─────

More evidence of the Jungquists' trying to pull Louise away from him. **Gollum's plan for an attempt to escape or a suicide pact in even of a guilty verdict was seen in this portion of one of his letters:**

I am truly sorry I got so mad at you but Do you realize that if we are found guilty, I get killed? I don't want to die. I want to live for you, honey. That is why the knowledge of the layout of that part of the jail is so necessary.

(He then asked her to draw him a diagram of her jail quarters and how he could reach them).

"If we have to do that thing, we'll only have one chance. No more. And we'll have to make good the first time."

Gollum made several references to their trial and probable verdict. For the most part he expressed confidence of acquittal but in some parts of his letter he wrote:[28]

> We will be acquitted, my darling. I hope we will be. I hope against hope that we will be found not guilty.
>
> I just saw Kaufman. He says Jacobs isn't as confident as he is. He thinks or is trying for a 10-year sentence. He (Kaufman) thinks the prosecution is going to prove I did it and we are so much in love that you are standing by me regardless. He is pretty sure of an acquittal.
>
> I asked him about this not getting married on the 30th of April. He said that Jacobs had talked you into it and if I asked you, you would say yes any time I wanted you to. (Am I right?)
>
> He said he couldn't at the moment see a great deal of legal reason, or strategic reason for us not getting married. However, he is going to think it over and talk about it with Dr. Holder and others with my, and your, interests at least.
>
> He thinks the judge would have to OK it too.
>
> If my parents and the attorneys think it's OK and the judge gave his consent and all, would you marry me April 30th even against the desires of your uncles?

On the other hand, the girl wrote:

> I'm only worried about the verdict. And whether I can hold out missing you so. Darling, I've been trying to imagine life without you. It doesn't work.

In his next letter, Gollum urged that Miss Overell insist on marrying him, that it might look good to public eyes. Evidence that the two families are in different corners.

---

28 The papers mention of this passage, which is displayed in the copy of the original handwritten note, was not included in reproductions taken from the Examiners' article and suggests that the paper did not include all the notes in their possession. It is included in this document as taken from the handwritten note itself.

Saturday 3:07 PM

*I just saw the parents. They think the best thing to do would be to get a court order to get married on the 30*th *of April.*

They are reminding you of the fact that your Grandmother's estate enters into this case also. The general impression is that your relatives don't want you acquitted – and Mom and Pop both said, **insist** *and insist again that you want to marry me.*

It might do more good as expression of faith, in the public's eyes than any possible harm. But don't forget, you'd have to **insist** *and insist and insist again. If this order comes through would you insist on marrying me? (I have never asked you a more important question, you know, except one, and you said yes, then).*

My dear baby, I love and adore you and I want you to say yes. But consider all the angles and everything carefully. Then, if you say yes, I'll know that it is without reservation. Without doubt in your mind.

Now, wait a minute, remember that if you are found guilty, of anything, you will lose the estate. It will go to your uncles and your grandmother. Then your grandmother's estate would go only to them. Even if your mother and father were mentioned in the will because you would be ineligible. I sure hope you are going to say yes to that question and insist. I have tried to be impartial but I still want you and need you and love you and adore you and want you to say yes.

Is this right? Where is the door to the kitchen into your place? Where is the elevator?

I love you my dear. I adore you. I would very much like to know about the way from your cell to the elevator. All the doors and what kind, etc. (Bells, buzzers, etc.) Will you please also take notice if any of the male guards open any doors up there?

Take note of the matron's habit. Does she sleep in that room? Is there a buzzer that rings telling her to open the door when a girl is brought up? Or do they call up from below stairs? Please notice all these little things possible, my little baby dear.

Do you mind if I call you Baby or Baby Doll? How about after you have a baby or six, will you mind me calling you baby then? We will have many, many, children, dear and they will all be beautiful like you.

Please, oh please, don't forget me. Don't leave me. I love you. If you were to leave me, there would be no reason for me to live. Without your love, I am nothing. We will be married and live together and work together for the rest of our lives.

I love your eyes, your lips, your nose, your ears, your beautiful face, your wonderful neck. Oh my darling, my wonderful beautiful dearest baby, I love you.

I can (will) contain myself until after the trial is over. But not any longer. Then I am going to claim you as my bride. And I pray you will still want to claim me as your husband.

Please want me to be your husband. Remember me? I'm the guy you're going to marry and love and cherish until death does us part. And old man death is about 80 years away for both of us.

—————

Saturday 4-12-47

Baby mine,

First an apology for last night's note. I'll explain that.

Remember how you felt about that telephone conversation with Miss Ricks that time at your house? Well, I felt that way last night.

Remember that remark you made that Mr. Jacobs might be a competitor if he liked me?

Does that mean it's all up to him?

(Inaccessible) Jacobs is afraid on about that. After this there will be no references to our case or to any of those things suspicious to them. Just little notes saying I love you. Just so you'll know that I'm alive and well and in love with you.

You do love me you say. The papers had it spread over them too. So even if they start reading the notes, so what? If you ever leave me, I'll sue you for breach of promise.

My baby darling dearest one, I adore you. Your lovely hair (inaccessible)....

Gollum denies in this following letter that he was after Miss Overell's money. He even proposes to renew an agreement to that effect.

4-13-47 8:30 AM

27th day in jail

47 days to trial

My Baby Dear,

I love you. I adore you. I want you. All the time I want you.

Geemonie Chrismus—I thought you knew my parents better than to think they would be after your money. And as far as I'm concerned, I wish you would have Mr. Jacobs draw up a paper (this would suffice so you might keep it), something like this:

I, George Rector Gollum, for the consideration of one dollar ($1) already received, do hereby release and absolve Miss Beulah Louise Overell, my future lawful wife (inaccessible).

(Inaccessible) Louise (?) Gollum to retain the complete management and title to and of all said property. Investing and reinvesting her profits and earnings thereof to her own advantage and desires provided further that they not be conferred in any way on the said George Rector Gollum, her future lawful husband.

By my hand signed and sealed this 13th day of April, 1947.

GEORGE RECTOR GOLLUM

The prosecution, I understand, has not any motive as yet, for us. As I understand. As I see it, their whole case hinges on connecting us or me directly with the dynamite and our being the last people on board.

I've been thinking that they might try to say that I did it and you love me so much you are shielding me.

The guy I'm getting the money from is an ex-shipmate of mine who I lent money when together in the navy. He is an "Okie" and oil has opened up on his land. He is putting aside a certain percentage for me. Just because I lent him that money in the navy.

I am sure glad that no one could talk you out of marrying me. I thought that they couldn't and now that you say so, why I sure am happy.

*If we are married in here, why then I want you to go straight home with me. But if we are not married by the end of the trial, why, I want you to leave with me **not more** than hour after the jury says not guilty. We will then go to Nevada or Arizona and be married, stay there overnight and then come back here to get our personal property.*

I love you, my dear one. I adore you. My love is yours for now and eternity. There is no one else. There will never be anyone else. I worship and (inaccessible)…

We sure will be acquitted, (I hope). If we aren't, then our life insurance goes into effect. Now I imagine you know what our life insurance is. N'est ce pas?

I'll spend the rest of my life trying to make you the happiest person on the face of the earth.

With all my love, your husband Popsie.

Friday, April 15
31 days in jail
33 days to trial

(Deleted) Mr. Jacobs to (delete). OK, so he is your lawyer. So you think he is a swell guy. I thought the four of us had an understanding that we would have a conference today. And why don't we? I'll tell you why. The illustrious Mr. Jacobs is in Los Angeles. That's why.

He might have had to go. He might have had something really important. But (deleted) it. He could have at least told Mr. Kaufman he was going. He could have at least let Mr. Kaufman know there was to be no conference today.

All week I dream of this day. I lie on my bunk and dream of seeing you, of holding you in my arms, of kissing you. I dream of hearing your voice. I dream (inaccessible)….

We will be married. *If you leave me, I would kidnap you and force you to marry me. They have told you it would be better not for us to get married until after the trial. Well, maybe that is good legal strategy. I hope so. But I am going to marry you within six hours after the trial is over.*

The foreman of the jury will come in and say, "We the jury find the defendants not guilty." There will be much yelling and stuff. And then we will have to come back over here and pick up our personal property and stuff.

Both talk of sleeping pills.

You said that if I was unfaithful to you, you would take an overdose of sleeping pills. You need never have to do that. I will never be unfaithful to you.

And I am promising you now by means of this letter, that if you ever leave me or are unfaithful to me, or stop loving me, I will take that overdose of sleeping pills. After I have killed the man you turned to from me. That is a promise.

My life is in your hands. That is not just an irrational thought. (Inaccessible) OUR EMOTIONS STRIPPED NAKED BY THE COLD PROBING EYES OF THE JURORS, THE COLD SENSATION LOVING PUBLIC AND THE MERCILESS HOUNDING OF THE PROSECUTORS.

My dear baby, I just got your replies from my last two notes. The heat deal is about these notes (inaccessible) The guard who is carrying them (inaccessible). So I won't be able to write for a few days. I don't even know if he will be able to take this one off. Maybe in a few days.

With the perhaps good news we were hearing today that our chances of acquittal are improving each day. But if I don't have your love and faith and trust after we are acquitted, if by then you have decided that you have had enough of me then there would be no use of MY BEING ACQUITTED. I see that you have been thinking of (some of them anyway) that I wrote. I AM AFRAID THAT YOU MIGHT GET AWAY TOO. Or be gotten away in some manner. Don't you see after the trial that your custodians could force you to get in an auto and whisk you to a place where I could not find you for many months? I do not want that to happen. I repeat what I've said before. I trust none but you. No one. Bar nobody. I trust you and you alone.

And here you don't even trust me. I guess you must trust somebody else. Who? Mr. Jacobs. I don't trust him or Mr. Kaufman either—not *completely. I think in a way that your getting that money is too damned bad. Before you had it, you weren't so worried about me marrying you for your money. And now you are worried about that fact. Be damned to your money. Give it away. Give it to some charity or something. I want you and I want you without any doubts in your mind.*

I am going to marry you. You are going to marry me even if you don't love me. You can kick and scream and beat at me and curse me and anything else.

I wish we were man and wife right this minute. This second. Even through all this tirade, I know beyond doubt that we will be married and live the rest of our lives happily after we are acquitted.

I'm sure beginning to hate the word money. And I mean hate. Everywhere I turn to, it is money! Money! Money! Money! Money! You aren't the only one who keeps telling (inaccessible) I am trying to marry you (inaccessible).

_____

More evidence of family infighting.

I just saw Kaufman. He says he "isn't sure whether we should get married right away or not."

I love you my dear. I adore you with all my heart and soul. I miss your voice, I miss your presence, I miss you. I do so wish you were with me right now. I wish we were in our own home alone. That's why I don't want to have a housekeeping couple living in a house of ours. We wouldn't have complete freedom.

I miss you. I want to be with you. On a blanket in the woods under a tree. Or on the beach at night with the waves sighing on the sand. Just you and I alone as nature intended us to be.

My dearest, I get a thrill every time I hear your voice. Every time your beautiful mind is working. When you talk to me and discuss your ideas, I get a wonderful pleasure from it. My dearest baby doll, I love you to pieces.

Hey baby, about this relation business, I don't give a (deleted) if you think your relatives are the best in the world and mine are the worst or vice versa. Or what I think of both sets of relatives.

I am marrying YOU and YOU are marrying me. I ain't marrying your (deleted) relatives and you aren't marrying my (deleted) relatives – any of them. So nuts to them all. As soon as we are married and together, we won't have any relatives from either side. Just acquaintances, no more no less. Period. I want you right now my dear. Free and married right this instance. I do so much wish that we were.

We would be right now if that (deleted) chief of police Hodgkinson and Sheriff Music hadn't gotten (inaccessible)

Made in the USA
Charleston, SC
11 June 2013